RAISED BY NARCOTICS

Growing Up in the Opioid Epidemic

a memoir

RAISED BY NARCOTICS

Growing Up in the Opioid Epidemic

a memoir

ALYSE NEIBAUR

Raised by Narcotics: Growing Up in the Opioid Epidemic
Copyright © 2019 by Alyse Neibaur

All rights reserved. No part of this publication may be reproduced, stored in or introduced into a retrieval system, or transmitted, in any form, or by any means electronic, mechanical, printing, recording or otherwise, without the prior permission of the author and/or publisher.

Author Photo by Camera Shy

Edited by Julie Swearingen (www.julieswearingen.com)
And Keith Gordon (www.consmicedit.com)

Cover Design and Interior Typesetting by Melissa Williams Design
Cookie Images Copyright ©2019 New Africa, Shutterstock; Drugs and Pills ©2019 Peterfactors, AdobeStock; Prescription papers ©2019 dolva, AdobeStock

Special credit to @UtahSatire on Facebook

ISBN: 978-0578463063

Published by Bottled Up Foundation, LLC
bottledupfoundation.org; facebook.com/groups/bottledup
Bottled Up Foundation logo designed by Erik Neibaur

www.alyseneibaur.com
Instagram and Facebook: @AuthorAlyse

For Jane, Teresa, and Diane

AUTHOR NOTE

I have done my best to give you an accurate telling of events that have occurred in my life. These events are colored in my own emotion and perspective and any truth I share is subjective. While all the stories in this book are true, some names and identifying details have been changed to protect the privacy of the people involved.

The only permanent truth is death.

CHAPTER 1

Social Media

I find myself opening Facebook for what must be the thousandth time today. I might be a little addicted—and not even to my own friends (if you can call them that), but to the pages I follow that share stupid memes, GIFs, and videos. I waste a sizeable portion of my life staring at my phone without any discernable reason, just throwing minutes, and hours, of my life away. On this particular day, I come across the Utah Satire page—it's one of my favorites, and 99% of the time I find it absolutely hilarious. It's full of jokes or memes about Mormons and Utah culture in general. It's so funny to me because I've grown up here, despite my constant daydreaming that I could escape. I've always hated Utah, although as I've become an adult I realize it's not Utah I hate—it's the people. But I wonder, do I just hate *people*? Am I just so shy and introverted that I would have an equal distaste for all people no matter where I go? I honestly don't know if I'll ever be able to answer that. I don't think people are bad, I just don't like to be around any of you. These social platforms, for me at least, seem to make these daily interactions more manageable. I can still be included in your daily life even if I never show up.

Which is another reason why I love the Utah Satire page. We all can have a good laugh at our neighbors without having to spend time with them. Because, let's face it, we've all seen it. We get it. It's hilarious and, like, "so true!" The Mormons really do love their green Jell-O, all my friends are addicted to Diet Coke, and my favorite condiment is fry sauce. No joke. Hahaha!

This was the post of the day:

> **Utah Satire:**
> *Post one thing Utahans can't live without!* (attached a photo of an old school game show host holding his mic out to his contestant.)
>
> **First Commenter (aka: game show contestant):**
> *Diet Coke and prescription painkillers!* *laughing-so-hard-I'm-crying emoji*

This first commenter was followed by jokes about funeral potatoes, driving badly, judging people, at-home pyramid scheme businesses, having eighteen children, and much more. We could all have a good laugh over these Utah stereotypes—except this time, I'm not laughing. Instead, I'm scrolling the comments. A few give me a quick chuckle. But I'm counting. I'm counting how many have liked that first painkiller comment or posted their own comment about painkillers.

RAISED BY NARCOTICS—Social Media

There are a lot. A few have added their own sad-face-with-a-tear emoji, and I debate adding my own. For many of us watching this thread there is so much truth in these comments that it's literally painful—and on such a deep level that we can't even express ourselves fully. There is nothing adequate. Even our words would fall on deaf ears, and all we're left with is a stupid little teary-eyed emoji. What can we say? We get the joke; we understand the stereotype. It's funny because it's true, but it hits so close to home that suddenly you can't breathe. Suddenly you want to find all those people laughing-until-they-cry and punch them in their little emoji noses!

Why don't you see how funny that is!

A tear falls from my eye.

What the people commenting on this Facebook thread don't know—what they will never know from a stupid laughter emoji—is that my family is dead, and no amount of commenting or social media-style therapy will bring them back. What would my family think of all this, anyway? How painful would it have been for them to see these types of discussions online? Their deepest regret in life, whittled down into a joke on social media.

It has taken me years to get to this point in my writing. I've started and restarted this book dozens of times. I've even written the entire thing in the form of a journal entry. An angsty diary where no one understands my pain, and I wish either I could die, or everyone around me could die. The pain is ceaseless, unending, forever. It runs deep and feels maddening. I am completely off my rocker, I'm a lunatic. I've gone off the deep end, I'm obsessed with something that no one can fix. I can't bring them back from the dead. Everything around me is broken, and I'm sitting in a pile of ashes with people all around me reaching their hands out to save me, and I sit here stubbornly trying to sift through the tiny pieces of burnt nothingness. I'm trying desperately to put together an image of something that might resemble anything close to what I went through, or what I once had. No one knows how I got here, how I came to sit in my ashy remains—the rubble that everyone just wants to pull me out of and sweep off to the side—but I want to make them see what my life once was. My hands are filthy. My focus is entirely on this and nothing else. I can't sleep, I can't breathe because it fills my lungs with every breath. I'm afraid to cry, to dampen and ruin what's been left to me. I am in charge now, no one else. I am left with this huge responsibility to piece it all back together, make something out of the ashes of the lives of the people that have disintegrated around me, and show the world what a mess we've made.

I'm a mother now. A wife. I have a family. A family I'm afraid I'm neglecting. A family that I pull into because the rest of the world doesn't understand me, but neither do these children or this man who has struggled for years to have a normal relationship with the woman he saved from a bad situation. He admitted to me that he thought it was something that could be fixed and let go. Something that could be set aside and forgotten. Am I hurting him by wishing he could understand too, knowing full well that he never will? What about my children? They play too many video games, I don't spend enough time with them, and I'm here wasting my life writing words the world will never see or care about.

What am I doing?

I'm passionate about a thing that I wish I didn't care about. I don't have to write this. I don't have to care about it. I can move on. I can raise my family, go on vacations every summer, work only because I'm bored, not because I'm broke. I can sip too many lattes, fill my time at the gym, and judge my friends for their lack of discipline and unhealthy lifestyles.

I'm rich. I'm bored. I'm an entitled millennial. I don't have to give one shit about any of this. They're dead. There's nothing I can do. I can live freely and be whoever I please! I can learn from their mistakes and laugh-until-I-cry emoji at every stupid Utah stereotype that I've lived through. Hahahahaha! It's so goddamn funny because it's true!

Originally, I was going to write this book like I'm a person the world knows and you all care enough about my story to read it. The problem with that is—and I've only just discovered this through my own readings of the book *The Subtle Art of Not Giving a Fuck*—that you probably don't care enough about your own damn self to read a book about the snooze fest of my life's story. Why should you care? I don't expect you to, and that's why I haven't been able to finish what I've started over and over and over again.

What do you care about? You care about fixing your life. You care about what you believe in, having your words heard, and not falling flat all over the ass-cracks of Facebook or Twitter. People don't care about you anymore than they care about me, but we all care about something—and well, unfortunately, this is my something.

I have to stop trying so hard and just get these words out.

I had stumbled on a Facebook post on a page I follow, and it made me want to hide in my bedroom and cry to myself. It reminded me that I've lost everything I ever knew, and now I take everything around me for granted. It reminded me that I'm weak and unable to hold myself together, even though someone was only joking around.

I've gotta do something about this.

CHAPTER 2

Self-Help

The last time someone in my family died was 2012. In the years since then, I've really worked on myself. I've done some awesome things. I got a job working with my best friend—something we had both been dreaming about for, well, forever. I started focusing on my health and what I'm putting into my body. I started running and signing up for races, even longer ones like half marathons. I lost weight (fifty pounds), shed numerous dress sizes, gained all kinds of self-confidence. I had another baby, my second, who is my entire world. I totally rocked motherhood and did everything for that little man to make sure he exceeded his own personal hang-ups and surpass them like nothing was ever wrong. I taught my daughter what a strong and independent woman looks like and helped her become the independent woman she is now growing into. I saved money for our ten-year wedding anniversary, so my husband and I could go rekindle our love on the island of Hawai'i—where we were lucky enough to honeymoon—

and revisit all those wonderful feelings we share for each other.

Life has been good. I've made a lot of good choices. I don't regret most of it—it's what everyone loves about me. This is how everyone sees me: my "friends" on Facebook, my family, the people I work with, even the people I grew up with. I'm strong and capable, and alongside my husband, we have a life that anyone would be envious of.

My life is a fairytale.

But—and you saw this part coming, right—just like a fairytale, my life is not what it seems. I mean, it is *actually* everything I described. I did have all that, but *why* anyone has what they have is a question no one asks. We all just assume that everyone has more than we do, and poor us for not having what they have.

Choices. We make them every single day. In my case, I would like to think that I have what I have now because I've worked hard for it. I am who I am because I wanted something very specific for my life, and that meant being a very specific type of person. But what drives people to make these choices? Why are we all so possessed to create this stable life for ourselves, a life that everyone envies?

Self-help is so popular right now because we all so badly want to be in charge of our own destiny. There is a huge problem with this, though—because the truth is, we can't be. I wish I could say that everything I've done, I've done alone. I really wanted to be that independent woman that so many women pride themselves in being, but they are lying to themselves if they think they are independent.

RAISED BY NARCOTICS—Self-Help

Everything we do will always revolve around another person, or an experience with another person. I can never truly be independent unless I purge myself of everything I know, every single possession that I have—including the clothes on my back—and live alone in the wilderness, making, building and growing everything on my own.

You are not independent.

You might be alone, but you are not independent.

That doesn't have to be good or bad. It is what it is. We all rely on each other. Very heavily at times, while at other times we might not even realize it. I credit my husband's job for a lot of things that we have and are able to do. Without that company, their family-friendly environment, and their benefits, we just wouldn't be who we are. Who we are is very much a reflection of how well they've built their company. But you don't want things like this to be true. You want to think that you would be who you are no matter what happened to you, but you wouldn't be. Each and every circumstance of your life shapes you somehow. Every job, every friendship, every meal, every event. You would not be who you are without having experienced everything that has come to you—good or bad—in your life. You will not be the same person when you're done reading this book.

Take the old adage: "You knew who I was when you married me." This statement is a personal pet peeve of mine. Well, yeah, they knew who you were the day they married you, but you've changed, in a lot of little ways. So, no, you are not the same person—and if you are the same person, you've done something very wrong with your life.

You haven't grown, you haven't learned, you haven't experienced anything new. Believe it or not, your loved ones *want* to know you—you just have to let them in, and start recognizing the ways life has changed you.

I want to be a specific type of person, but I don't actually know who that person is yet. Everything in my life has been an accident, followed by a choice I've had to make. An invitation by a friend, a benefit of being part of something bigger than me, a book recommendation, forgetting to cancel my Audible membership, a diagnosis, a canceled event, a surprise night out—the list goes on. Nothing I've done to make me who I am has been deliberate, except for one thing.

But defining and explaining that one thing is the difficulty and point of this entire book. What I *do* know are the mistakes that my family made in the past, and what it ultimately cost them—their lives. I also know that I don't want to make those same mistakes, so I've focused my attention on things that will make me a better human being. When those particular opportunities for growth present themselves, I nosedive for them, actively avoiding the things in my way that might have once tempted my long-lost family members, but not me. I won't be tempted, because I'm better than they were—or so I keep telling myself.

That's all it is, simply knowing that I don't want to be like them. Instead, I've ended up like me. That doesn't make me better or worse—it just gives me a way to be different, because I don't want to be the same. As a mother, my mantra has been: "I don't know what to do, but I know what

RAISED BY NARCOTICS—Self-Help

not to do." This has come from my experiences with my own mother, a person who really had no idea what she was doing in the arena of motherhood. That comparison alone gave me something to lead my family with.

I have no idea what I'm doing in this life, but I sure as hell know what I'm not doing.

And that is how I've become the person that I am today, to live this fairytale lifestyle that everyone around me envies. It's not always about knowing what you're doing, but rather knowing what you're not doing. The biggest example of this, in my own life, is drugs.

Drugs are bad, 'mkay.

I don't just mean street drugs—although they're certainly included in this. I mean prescription drugs, because that's what this book is ultimately about (if you didn't already catch that drift from the first paragraph of the book).

But how can you possibly say no to prescription drugs? It's impossible. Even I can't avoid them. I would be a hypocrite if I said that I did. I feel like I need to start telling my story now, though, so you can catch up on the meaning of all this. It's not meant to be a mystery, or some puzzle to be solved. I really want my words to make an impact, and I've waited too long already. There are kids just like me living this same hell right now, and they could be helped if I could just finish what I started so many years ago. So many families have already gone through this, and so many people are going through it now. I still don't know what I'm doing, what I'm writing, or what will happen when I'm done—I just know that I can't sit by anymore and let it keep happening without saying something. I can't not speak up and tell my own story.

No one is laughing anymore, because we all know someone going through something similar to what I'm about to share with you. I recognize that you don't know who I am or what I've been through, but I know that you care about someone in your life—and if anything, this could be a turning point for both of you.

CHAPTER 3

Opidemic

You know those fun mash-ups they make up for celebrity couples? Bennifer, Brangelina, Kimye? Let me share a fun mash-up you may not have heard of: Opidemic.

So, what the hell does Opidemic mean?! If you live in Utah, you know exactly what it means, and it's about as stupid as the combined celebrity names making their rounds across social media. Opidemic is derived from Opioids and Epidemic, a fun little catchy word to help us millennials wrap our heads around what's happening in our own backyard. An opioid epidemic. Because we were not capable of understanding that otherwise. Not quite as fun as Brangelina. LOL.

What is with this generation?

I wonder who decided to coin that word, because I would love to understand what went through their head when they decided it was okay. Let's have a conversation, you and me, because there is an entire website dedicated to this word that you created, and I can't decide if I hate it or if I wish I had thought of it first. I should give credit where credit is due, and you now have my full and complete attention. The very first time I saw a billboard for it—2016, I think—I was triggered with a flood of emotion and all I wanted was a safe space to hide, exactly as you may have intended. Having a meltdown while driving down I-15 was not an option. I think my husband was in the car with me, and let me tell you how hard it was trying to explain my sudden silence to a man who knows me very well and knows when I've been set off internally. Like a little bomb imploding inside of my organs, he can hear it, smell it, see it. He knows. "Nothing, dear," was the best I could muster, but I kept seeing the image in my head and all the other images that went along with it. You guys are good, and I hope it's helped someone. But billboards are probably as effective as the "You Should Fear Death" billboards to instill the fear of God—and thus the belief—into you.

Because not believing in God is a sin, and some billboard is going to convince me of that?

When I see those God-fearing billboards, I can't help but think of the Davy Jones monster from Pirates of the Caribbean, asking the crew, "Do you fear death?" It's a little too late for that question to help the members of my family who are now buried six feet under. I suppose they didn't fear death, but I'll never get the chance to ask them.

I'm actually pro-Opidemic, if that surprises anyone—at least the term. I was all about that message, but what I really felt was angry. Angry that it wasn't there when I needed it most.

RAISED BY NARCOTICS—Opidemic

Where the hell were your giant posters when I was going through hell with my family?

At the time, I thought that whoever came up with those slogans and billboards was also going through hell with their own family, but I've since learned that it's actually run by the Utah Department of Health, which includes doctors, bureaucrats, and real people struggling with their families. People who are having to watch patients, loved ones, and friends die. No matter how the opioid epidemic touched our lives, it is affecting all of us.

In hindsight, this situation is a terrible bitch. You can't help but think about all the things you wish you could've done differently, things you realize only after the fact. I wish I had written this book sooner. I wish I could get over myself—and the misconceptions everyone has about me and my lifestyle—and just throw these words onto a page so that people could get the help they need sooner rather than later. Too late for my family. Too late for their family. All they are anymore are statistics. What good are statistics?

Before we go any further, we need a little history. So, what is an opioid anyway? First, we need to understand that we have opioid receptors all throughout our bodies. They exist all throughout our nervous system and gastrointestinal tract, which basically translates to our brain, spine, and intestines. This actually accounts for a large percentage of our body. Second, opioids are substances that reduce pain and alter the reactions of these receptors. It's important to note that opioids should only be taken in the short term, because over time our bodies can become dependent on them and no longer respond properly without them. Thank you, WebMD.

Science is incredible. It's just mind-blowing to think how medicine interacts with every single tiny little piece of our bodies. That we even have such a substance to relieve our own physical discomfort is just astounding, let alone the fact that we can understand, with a simple internet search, how it all works. If you have time, totally Google that shit. It's crazy.

Opioids themselves are not the problem. Much like the sentiment that "guns don't shoot people, people shoot people," drugs don't kill people, people kill people—yet we blame opioids for the death of over 125 people each day across this nation. That amounts to tens of thousands of deaths per year, but doctors and policymakers still can't agree on that statistic because there's disagreement as to what constitutes a drug overdose as opposed to, let's say, a stroke.

We, all of us—doctors, patients, pharmacy techs, and particularly in regard to this book, the medical industry as a whole—makes a choice every single day that affects so much more than just ourselves. I have to ask: who's responsible? The drugs are not going to hop into your body and kill you. A venomous spider might bite you and kill you, but drugs can't do that. Only you and your doctors, and the folks at Big Pharma, can make the decision that you are going to become a drug addict. It's in their best interest to become an addict—and they will try to convince you that it's in your best interest, too. There is quite a bit of

RAISED BY NARCOTICS—Opidemic

psychological manipulation at play here. It's a long and disgusting chain of that old childhood game of Telephone. You know, the one where children stand in a line side-by-side, the first child whispers something into the next child's ear, and as they continue down the line the message becomes morphed into something else entirely. The original message most likely gets lost altogether. Now, let's say that a pharmaceutical company creates several different drugs. Some of these drugs take off, and doctors can sell them very easily, because, well, they work. "Here, take my money."

Other drugs, for whatever reason, aren't as appealing to doctors. So along the message-line, not only are doctors being persuaded psychologically via sales pitches and seminars that may be a bit misleading, but they are also incentivized to create a catchier message to sell more drugs. This is how the opioid epidemic began. Before the pills ever reach your medicine cabinet, an entire line of misleading, manipulative, and incredibly persuasive incentives were built into the very foundation to make sure that you too can become a drug addict.

Who can you even trust?

Perhaps the telephone game is a terrible metaphor. I think of it as a line of people the drug itself must pass through, and along that line each person is given a different incentive ($$) to tweak the message to make the drug seem more appealing. Using catchy phrasing to mislead you, and even your doctors. They are, after all, the very people putting it into your hands. They need to be persuaded before you are that it's worth the investment. Now let's start to think of this as an investment. A product. Don't you want to invest in your own health?

Ah, see, there it is.

Trust is so important, but when it comes right down to it, sometimes you can't even trust yourself (and I know from personal experience). Trusting your doctor is literally putting your life into their hands, but you wouldn't put your life into say, your stylist's hands, would you? No, that's stupid. All they know how to do is cut hair. I'm a licensed cosmetologist, by the way, so this is a fun example for me. As a cosmetologist, we were trained less in how to cut or style hair—that all comes from on-the-job experience—and more on how to sell product. Our job requirements included how much we had to sell, in solid numbers; our performance was based on how well we moved products off our shelves and pushed it into the hands of our clients. Let me tell you, your doctors are trained to do the exact same thing with medication. Every single clinic or hospital in the country bases the performance of their entire staff on their ability to put drugs into your hands, because drugs are their product. Their entire job is to convince you that you need it.

Let me give you a bit of an example. Our jobs as stylists was to use the product in your hair while you were sitting in our chairs, and while we were doing our thing, we would be actively trying to convince you of just how amazing the product was (and, of course, we were paid a commission on every product that walked out the door). No difference with doctors. None. Perhaps they are paid to promote the product vs. making a commission on a per item basis, but that is the only distinction to be made. This example makes me feel a little sick because of my experience in beauty school, and actually being handed little slips of paper from our instructors with the big RX in the corner. They very literally taught us how to "prescribe" solutions for different types of hair our clients had. Let me ask you this, though: when did your hair ever NEED these products? I can tell you that that aspect of my job was incredibly difficult for me as a stylist—and I was just a stylist. Can you even imagine the pressure doctors are under, and the ethics involved in working in the business of killing you? I can't.

I'm starting to sound like a hippy out of one of those documentaries that I love to watch. I'm not trying to scare you, I'm trying to educate you and put the choices back into your hands, not in the hands of doctors and pharmaceutical reps. You're going to feel trapped, pressured—and you should, because it's your life and your health on the line. You must find a way to educate yourself. The thing is, none of this is a secret. I'm not blowing anyone's minds by saying this stuff. This is the truth we have all come to know and somehow accept. I just want to ask you: are you really okay with it? Because I'm not. That's why I'm writing, because I'm not okay with it. When I got swept up in it, I was just a child, trusting everyone around me, not knowing any better—but now that I'm an adult, my biggest fear is that my children will be too trusting. It cost my ignorant family their lives, and I didn't know any better to help them stop it. Conversely, I now trust no one at all. I think everyone around me has a shady agenda—I just have to choose which agenda I'm okay being a part of. That's not a happy existence, but that is the definition of existing. You get to choose your demons. You will die, someday—the question is: how much control do you want over how it happens?

As you may have gathered, I'm a huge proponent of choices. If your goal in life is to be a happy addict on the streets with no family or money, and you like it that way, who's to say that's bad? If you're not inflicting pain onto others, no harm no foul, am I right? If you want to do that with your life, own it. You be you.

But what I know about human nature, however, is that while there might be the occasional oddball who wants that kind of life—truly *wants* it—the other 99% of the human population wants something better. We all have dreams, goals, hopes. We all want something better than what we have right now.

So, I ask the question: what the hell are we doing to each other?

CHAPTER 4

Family Tree

One day in 2016, my daughter Aryn came home from school. I think she was in third or fourth grade at the time, and she had a fun paper she had done representing her family tree. She wanted to show it to me and pulled it out of her backpack as she unloaded all her school work onto the kitchen counter. Now, if I'm being honest, how often do I *really* pay attention to the details of any paper she hands me after school? Not very much. Usually I can just nod at her and say, "Great job, Aryn," or "That looks awesome!" She'll be satisfied and on her way, then to the recycling can it goes. Lost to the world, and into the heaps of trash along with our other material possessions.

This time, however, I looked. I took in the detail. I praised her for doing a great job filling it in, and inside of my heart a little pain sprouted. A pain I did not know had been planted—yet there it was, growing. And with each passing second, it grew a little larger until I realized just what that pain really was. It was the knowledge that no one on my side of the family was anywhere on her family tree. Not even her Uncle Cody, who was very much still alive.

There was me, of course, and her father Shawn. There was Grandma Jo and Grandpa Ray, Shawn's parents. There was Aunt Holly, Shawn's sister, and Uncle Scott, Shawn's brother. There was even Aunt Alicia, Shawn's oldest sister who we almost never visited, even though she lived just down the street. I suppose we talked about her enough that Aryn remembered who she was and how she was related to us. There was Great-Grandma Joan, Grandma Jo's mom, but nowhere on this little paper was her Grandma Diane (Nana, as the kids called her) or her Grandpa Ben—but why on earth would he be on there? She didn't know him any better than I did, and he honestly didn't deserve a spot on this paper. No Uncle Cody, my brother, and no Great-Grandma Jane, my grandmother. Only Shawn's half of the family was present, which was to my little girl's perspective probably ninety-five percent of our family.

I muttered to myself, "Shit."

And the pain grew and grew and grew.

My little girl didn't know my side of the family. Her little toddler brother Nick wouldn't even have the early memories that Aryn might still remember if she thought hard enough about them.

I didn't know what to do about it.

* * *

As far as this book is concerned, what I decided to do was *write*. I decided that I needed to write about my family and

RAISED BY NARCOTICS — Family Tree

explain who they are. They were my entire world for so many years. I would do them (and myself) a great injustice if I didn't explain who my family was. Giving this background will also help clarify the rest of the story that is to come.

It starts with Grandma Jane and Grandpa Bill. These two were my grandparents on my mother's side. It's safe to say that I don't know my father, and consequently I don't know his side of the family, so we won't go there. Not yet, anyway.

Grandma Jane got pregnant out of wedlock sometime in the 50s and gave birth to my Uncle Karl. I don't know the story of Karl's father, or where the guy ended up. What I do know is that she met my Grandpa Bill sometime right around Karl's birth, and Grandpa Bill unofficially adopted him and raised him as his own. Grandma Jane and Grandpa Bill got married. All I have as evidence of this marriage is her cubic zirconia wedding ring, too small to fit on any of my own fat fingers. Grandma Jane was a good three inches smaller than me, and much more petite.

And so, the Nielsen clan began. Grandma Jane and Grandpa Bill went on to have three daughters. The oldest was Teresa, the middle daughter was Diane (my mother), and the third and youngest daughter was Sylvia.

I've heard many stories of their family dynamics. Of course, those dynamics bled into my own childhood, especially considering just how old my Mom was when she had her first child, Cody, and then me.

Mom had stories about living on a great deal of land where Grandpa Bill first built our family's home in Spanish Fork, Utah in the early 1970s. They had ducks and dogs, and she reminisced about going camping and fishing with him. She said that he was her best friend through this time in her young life. If I were to rewrite the story—for, what would it be now, the 8th time?—I would start here and highlight their friendship just before Mom's life truly began to unravel. Her story reaches as far back as my own does, when Grandma Jane and Grandpa Bill decided to get divorced when Mom was only twelve years old.

Memories, of course, are a tricky beast to deal with. What's true and what's not true? My story is not the same as Cody's story, is not the same as Mom's story, is not the same as Grandma Jane's story—and on down the line it goes. What I *can* tell you are the stories I've heard, so that we can begin piecing this huge puzzle together. Some of these stories are not going to be taken well if anyone on my side of the family reads this book, but if little Aryn's family tree assignment says anything, it's that I don't have a "my side" of the family. All I can do is take a deep breath and move forward.

After her parents split, Mom's life changed. How could it not? Divorce is not easy on a child, especially not when your very best friend suddenly moves out of the house.

Mom always told us that after the divorce, her life became a living hell. Now that Grandpa Bill was not there to protect her, her older half-brother Karl started taking out both his anger and his teenage hormones on her. Why

RAISED BY NARCOTICS—Family Tree

didn't he do this to Teresa or Sylvia? I can only assume it's because Teresa was basically a boy in her own right, with hobbies like wrestling and kissing girls, and Sylvia was the baby, several years younger than Mom and all too innocent and naïve.

Mom became terrified of her older brother, who she claimed started beating and molesting her at the tender age of twelve. Teresa quickly became her guardian, but if she could not be there because of after-school activities or some other obligation, Mom would hide in the closet under the stairs in the basement until Karl was gone—whether he was heading out to work, going on a date, or do something at church.

Where was Grandma Jane, you might ask? Working full-time at the diner on Main Street to support her young family. I've always felt that this information was incredibly relevant to the story of my mother's life. It makes later events make a lot more sense.

Grandpa Bill went on to marry a new woman, who was later known as the love of his life. I knew her as Grandma Erma, and I adored her. She wrote her own music and played the guitar. I still have the guitar that she played for us when we would visit. It's still sitting in my closet—I never learned how to play it, but she did inspire me enough to want to. Grandpa Bill and Grandma Erma didn't have any children together, but as the story goes, he helped her raise her children while he only occasionally visited his own. But at the very least, when I came along, I knew that blended side of the family as my own. They were just as much cousins, aunts, and uncles to me as any other. More distant, but still family.

The family tree continued growing only a few years later when Mom gave birth to her first child—a son named Cody, in 1977—when she was only fifteen-years-old. Aunt Teresa never had any children. In 1985, Aunt Sylvia married Michael, and both she and my mom became pregnant with girls around the same time. Aunt Sylvia gave birth to Amanda Jane—or Mandy as I know her—in June of '86, and one month later I came into the world to be Mandy's almost-twin and best-friend-forever. Mom named me Alyse, and I can't remember why—I think I was supposed to be Lisa, but whatever happened to change that, I don't know. For as long as I can remember, though, she didn't call my Alyse. My nickname has always been CeCe (see-see). I came up with the spelling years ago. I couldn't tell you where that came from. I have a theory, though, that sometimes she called me "Leasy," and Cody called me "sissy," and somehow it all blended into CeCe, and now that's how my family knows me. CeCe. It's as normal to me as Alyse. I'll respond to both. I won't lie, I enjoy my nickname quite a bit—sometimes I even prefer it.

Thankfully Mom stopped having children, and Aunt Sylvia later divorced Michael and married a man named Tim. Tim was the person I knew as my uncle. Uncle Michael was just the person who stole my best friend Mandy from me every summer for an entire week, and I hated him for it. Aunt Sylvia and Uncle Tim had two more children: Susanne Diane (named after Mom), or Susie, and

RAISED BY NARCOTICS—Family Tree

William, or Billy, named after Grandpa Bill. I wasn't particularly close to either of them. They were more like annoying younger siblings who occasionally tagged along behind me and Mandy. We all have a much better relationship these days.

While that was going on, Uncle Karl served a mission for the Church of Jesus Christ of Latter-day Saints, or the Mormon (or LDS) Church. I'm sure my Grandparents would have been proud of him for this, as they had all grown up attending church. There is a strong Mormon background to my Utah family—many of my ancestors came across the plains as pioneers for the Mormon Church, as is the case with many families here in this state. My own mother became an inactive member, as the term goes, after becoming pregnant with Cody. Teresa became inactive for her own reasons; Sylvia meanwhile remained active and went on to baptize her children in the church, although I don't think she was married in any of the temples. Both of my grandparents became inactive as well.

At the very least, I know that Grandma Jane still truly believed in the teachings of the LDS Church, but with everything that her family had been through, she stopped going. Essentially, she stopped trying to keep up with the Joneses. She smoked, drank coffee, and lived her life for herself—but on the first Sunday of each month, she would still tithe (or donate) some amount of money to the church, but only when she could afford it. I can't tell you her reasons for doing it. I can guess that she was trying to make something up to God for the sins of her family, but I could be far off base. Karl remained active in the church (despite his crimes against my mother), and when he came back from his mission, he proceeded to marry a beauty queen from our home town of Spanish Fork, April. Karl and April got married in one of the many temples we have here in Utah, and together they have five children. Their oldest is only one year younger than Cody, and their youngest is three years younger than me. I can't say that I was particularly close to any of them, only seeing them on holidays throughout the year.

Uncle Karl built for himself a small empire of farm land (and wealth) while the rest of us built something else entirely. This will become important later. Many people have two sides to their family. Mom's side and Dad's side. What we had was Karl's side of the family, and our side. The upper class, and the lower class, essentially. I'm certain even Uncle Karl saw it that way.

CHAPTER 5

It Was an Accident

I wasn't joking when I said that everything I am today is completely by accident. My life—from the very first cells forming in my mother's womb—is an accident. She didn't mean to get pregnant. She was just trying to have fun and be in love like so many of us are. Here I am, though, a product of that happy moment in her life before she knew she would lose it all. If she could tell you now, though, she would say we were the best parts of her entire life. I know this, and I am incredibly comforted by it.

That's life, isn't it? Just a series of accidents and our reactions to those accidents. The first ten years of my life were wonderful. Although we—Cody and I—grew up without our fathers, we had a relatively normal childhood. I mean, we both have stories that would make you question our mother's ability to raise children, or gasp in horror that a child could witness such an event—but I grew up in a loving home with two people who meant the world to me, and I meant the world to them. I played with Barbies, and had a few best-friends-forever, and celebrated every holiday at Grandma Jane's house with my cousins, never thinking "they have more than me" and never wanting more than what I had. Unless you count Disneyland, which was my biggest dream as a child. Thankfully, that finally came true at the age of nine when I got to go with my cousin Mandy. My mother busted her ass, saving her pennies so she could take us there, and it was magical. My childhood was fantastic. I wish I could go back, if even just to see my family smile again, hug them, and know that we were all okay. Happy, even. I believe my Mom was happy too, even if being a single mother is hard. I think she would agree with me that those ten years of life were the very best.

Those ten years ended too soon. Without warning, we were booted out of our home on Center Street in Spanish Fork, Utah—not because we couldn't afford the rent, but because the landlady's grandson wanted a starter home to share with his new wife. Unfortunately, it was the only rent we could afford, so we were suddenly without many options.

As I've sat trying to write this book a thousand times over again, I've really wanted to emphasize this moment because it was such a turning point in my life—and in all our lives. In the big picture, I guess it hardly matters—what matters isn't what we lost, it's where we went as a result of that loss. The only place we could go was to Grandma Jane's house.

She made room for us, because that's just what she did. It was a rhythm in life she was probably too familiar with:

RAISED BY NARCOTICS —It Was an Accident

bringing her adult children back into their family home. Mom had lived there on and off throughout her entire life, with and without my brother Cody. Grandma Jane was a second mother to us both, but this was the first time I would actually get to live with her.

My grandmother, Jane Diamond, was beautiful—just like her name implied—and as strong as a real diamond. Grandma Jane was the strongest woman I have ever met, and the woman I try to emulate in life. She was so strong that I never thought she could ever die. She seemed immortal, unflinching, unbreakable. The greatest force of nature I have ever met, who stepped in and stepped up whenever we needed her, and she raised me. How lucky am I?

Not only did we move in with her, but my Aunt Teresa lived there too. Teresa was also a force of nature—though an entirely different kind. While Grandma Jane was like the big trees sheltering you from the oncoming storm—not removing you from the wind and rain, but protecting you from it—Teresa was a volcano, temperamental and unpredictable. At a young age she had been diagnosed with bipolar disorder and schizophrenia. She was very easily sent spiraling off into turmoil, and often she was disconnected from reality and hallucinating about where she was, who she was, and who everyone else was around her. On the right medications, she was normal—or as normal as one really can be with that type of mental disorder. She couldn't hold down a job, even though she tried and failed several times before. She couldn't live on her own because she couldn't manage anything in her life. Grandma Jane was constantly her saving grace. Teresa would at times forget to take her medication—what we called her "crazy pills"—and you can guess that when she forgot, there was trouble. Not only was she mentally unstable, but she was an alcoholic. I have some interesting memories of visiting her in jail, watching her fall on the floor laughing hysterically after getting drunk, listening to her yell at my mother or Grandma Jane, but I was very young for most of those memories.

Mom and Grandma Jane tried to shelter me the best they could. When I looked at Teresa as a child, what I saw the majority of the time was a quiet woman who kept to herself, watched a lot of cable TV, and occasionally took me out for ice cream. When her behavior was controlled, she was my babysitter. She sat with me many times in Grandma Jane's basement while Mom was at work, playing Barbies, or Power Rangers, or coloring with me and applauding my artistic skill. She let me watch cartoons and gave me chocolate milk when I asked for it nicely. She was a fantastic aunt, and sometimes she said to me that I was like the daughter she never had.

Her life was interesting, and her existence in mine taught me many things about human nature, and the ability to find love no matter what your circumstances are. She loved deeply and only wanted that love in return. She was different, though, and too many people have a hard time with different. Not only was she mentally ill, but she was a lesbian. Not only was she a lesbian, but she wished she was a boy. She told me once, after I had asked her if she was a

RAISED BY NARCOTICS—~~It~~ Was an Accident

boy or a girl, that God had put her soul into the wrong body. She was supposed to be a boy but was sent into a girl's body. She only laughed with me when I asked (I think I was seven at the time). It was all in good fun, and she did her best to explain her opinions without feeling criticized. Never once did she take it personally—not when I asked stupid questions, and not when family shunned her because she was, in their eyes, a sinner. She knew who she was, and she owned who she was. She wouldn't (and couldn't) change for anyone around her, and she was just fine with it. Of all the people in the world who might feel self-conscious about who they are, to feel shame or embarrassment, she didn't feel an ounce of any of it. This inner strength has inspired me in so many uncountable ways in my life, even though she probably didn't even know that she had that strength to begin with. Sure, she was crazy, but she was a good person. I can't ever judge people for their circumstances after knowing a soul like hers.

Now I'm getting sentimental.

So far, I've told you about my Grandma Jane, and my Aunt Teresa, but not much about my own mother. Mom was a good woman. She did the best she could with the knowledge and tools at her disposal in the age of dead-beat-dads. She acted as both mother and father to Cody and me. She taught me about love and life, and she equipped me with a handful of life skills to take with me into the years to come. She did not censor herself around me, no matter my age. Through good and bad, I was the person she confided in, and she was mine. I say all of this with the nostalgia of a six-year-old girl. There seemed to be a completion between the two of us. Mom treated me as if I was the answer to all that life had thrown at her. I was her little miracle child that could do no wrong.

In the early days, Mom relied very heavily on both Grandma Jane and Aunt Teresa to take care of me while she worked, giving them the role of bonus mothers to me. I promise that I will delve into this more in the chapters to come, but right now, I have to explain what triggered our entire situation, and the reason for me to begin writing this book. It's been a thought in the back of my mind since my early teen years.

As you well know, everything in my life has been an accident. My birth, our move into Grandma Jane's house, and most importantly, the very thing that is impelling me to sit for hours on end writing this story: the car accident that changed everything in our lives.

We had lived with Grandma Jane and Aunt Teresa for a couple of years. We were settling into a routine but falling deeper into despair. Mom and Grandma Jane were always fighting over space, and I was being bullied at school. Nothing was much the same after we moved, and I started struggling with who I was and what this whole life really meant—something I'd never really struggled with before. Changing schools was a complete culture shock for me. I was not excited about leaving our little house, nor was I excited to move in with Grandma Jane and share a room with my mom, nor was I excited to leave my friends (who I only ever saw at school anyway). Where I was once actively

RAISED BY NARCOTICS—It Was an Accident

engaged with the world around me, now I was shy, quiet, and unsure of myself. The girls in my new fifth grade class picked up on this, and they used it against me. I think some things were unintended, as they are with children and the words that come out of their mouths. They were curious about me in a way I hadn't thought to be curious about myself. Why didn't I have a dad? Didn't I feel bad about that?

Other things were more intentional, however, and I was put through a minor case of fifth-grade hazing where they threatened not to play with me or be my friend if I didn't do what they said. The problem was, I didn't do what they said. They thought it would be funny to watch me pull someone else's hair, or steal someone's backpack or lunch, but I wouldn't (and couldn't) be part of that. I would not partake in their meanness, so I became friendless, a loner. This was the beginning of a downward spiral into what would become depression and anxiety.

I'd like to take a moment and say to those fighting for justice in the bullying department, keep fighting the good fight. Bullying is more complex than we tend to think. Things that adults might shrug off have the potential to feel world-ending to someone who is younger. One of my bullies had the decency to apologize to me a year later when we met again in middle school, but it was hardly enough to undo the damage that had already been done. As I entered middle school, I felt torn between two worlds: a world I had loved and been torn from, only to find out that my friends no longer needed or wanted me around; and the other world I had been thrown into, which caused me to feel terribly self-conscious about who I was and where I came from. I began to feel alone and out of place—and this was only the beginning.

I was eleven when we got the phone call. I was being lazy on the couch with a bowl of Doritos, watching some cartoon on Nickelodeon, when I heard Mom answer the phone. Immediately, I could hear that something was wrong. Grandma Jane and Teresa had been in a car accident. I can't recall much of the actual situation, or how we ended up at the hospital, but I distinctly remember going there right away.

They were at an intersection, waiting at a green light to turn left, when a driver who had fallen asleep at the wheel—a woman, if I remember right—tore through the intersection and struck their car on the passenger side, where Teresa was sitting. I've tried researching this accident to find out what happened to the driver. She lived, but no legal action was ever taken against her, or at least none that I'm aware of. What I do know is that this moment changed everything. A series of mistakes, of accidents leading to another accident, that shook our world and still impacts me to this very day, twenty plus years later.

The good news was that everyone survived. Grandma Jane walked away with only bumps and bruises. She sat with us, me and Mom, in the waiting room while Teresa, who was much less lucky, lay unconscious on an operating table.

We learned that the force of the impact twisted Teresa's passenger seat, breaking her spine in half as her body went from facing the front windshield to facing Grandma Jane's

RAISED BY NARCOTICS—It Was an Accident

seat. Her legs stayed in the forward position, but the entire upper half of her body twisted. I cringe every time I think about this. I cannot imagine that kind of pain.

What saved Teresa's life was that the accident happened right outside the hospital—they were waiting to turn left so she could meet her doctor for a mental health appointment. A series of accidents in one person's life, leading to life altering moments and accidents in another person's life.

CHAPTER 6

Diet Coke and Painkillers

What no self-help book can solve for you are the circumstances that are out of your control. And this situation was completely out of our control. All that we had control over was our choices, but again, not even a self-help book can guide you on the right choices to make in circumstances like this. A self-help book can't give you the money you need to make the best choices for your family, only the choice to decide how you feel about it. Financially speaking, this situation would knock any family to the ground, and it happened back in the mid-90s. Financial burden in the medical industry has only grown since then, not gotten better.

There's no pricing chart to decide what your best options are, so you're left to deal with the fallout. Nothing will prepare you for the moment the bill arrives and suddenly you owe thousands of dollars. What choices do you have in that situation?

RAISED BY NARCOTICS—Diet Coke and Painkillers

We had to first find out whether Teresa would ever walk again, or if the accident had paralyzed her. The doctors were dreary on this; they had little hope other than to say the break in her spine was clean—they at least gave us that to cling on to. But as I write this, I can't help but reflect on what their agenda might have been while explaining all our options to us. The tone in their voice really dictates how we respond to them, doesn't it? Their body language, their phrasing and word choice, the questions they asked... It's as if they had taken marketing classes and knew all the right ways to say, "This is your only option and here's why." It certainly feels as if you're being handed options. It feels as if you're in control, at least a little—but really, are you?

From this moment forward, I learned to ask a lot of questions, one of the most important being: "What questions should I be asking that I don't know about." I now want to get all perspectives of a given situation, and any and all answers I can possibly get. That is incredibly time-consuming, and some split-second decisions can't be helped. In this case, having my aunt Teresa sent into surgery immediately wasn't our choice, but one the doctors made on her behalf to help her survive the accident. This is why healthcare is so important, so that when your life is in someone else's hands, well, you get the best care you can without dying as a result.

We spent a lot of time with Teresa after her surgeries, watching the doctor do simple reflex testing on her joints and limbs to see if she could walk again. After a while, her feet began to respond to touch. She could feel. Small miracle.

Or was it?

I often wonder if being paralyzed without the ability to feel pain from the waist down would have been the better outcome for Teresa. Grandma Jane was now faced with an insurmountable decision. The first decision to put her on narcotic painkillers—Lortab, to be specific—was not a *decision* at all—it was a *prescription*. Do you ever question whether or not the prescription you're being handed is really the right choice? Do you ever ask how long will you be on it? Do you ask what the long-term solution for your pain will be? Take notes, write these questions down. You always want both short and long-term solutions.

But at the time, we didn't ask these questions. We didn't know we needed to. We were too focused on how to take care of her now that her life had changed so dramatically. She could no longer sleep in the same bed, so we needed a new hospital-type bed. She could no longer support her own weight, so she would need physical therapy. She would either need an in-home nurse, or be sent to a facility with people who were able to take care of her now-constant needs. Her meds would need to be strictly monitored, because no one knew how her mental health medication (like Lithium or Depakote) was going to interact with her pain medication (like Lortab, oxycodone, and/or morphine) and she couldn't very well stop taking the former.

Teresa's life was out of her control. She was being forced into a situation so beyond her comprehension that

RAISED BY NARCOTICS—Diet Coke and Painkillers

she likely didn't have a clue what was going on, or what her options were. Everyone around her talked about her as if she wasn't in the room. Some very important conversations happened when she wasn't even present at all. She was in pain, that's all she knew—and now she was exhausted because she was literally doped up on painkillers and couldn't keep up with anything happening to her or around her. She had to put her trust in the doctors and in her family. She had to put her trust in the eleven-year-old sitting wide-eyed at the foot of her hospital bed trying to keep up with the conversation happening between people three times her age.

Teresa's simple pleasures in life became Diet Coke and painkillers. She was strongly urged not to drink or smoke, but she continued smoking because why the hell not? What was the point to life if you couldn't enjoy it a little and relax with your personal habits and rituals? Her only happiness came in the form of sitting in her chair in the basement and being left to her vices.

Obviously, we couldn't afford to have her anywhere other than back at home. We all struggled with this solution, because we all had to help. Leading up to my twelfth birthday, Mom taught me how to take care of Teresa and delegated certain jobs to me so that I could help once I turned twelve. I would also be considered an in-home nurse by the state of Utah, so they would pay me for it. We had virtually no money to handle this situation, and the medical debt was piling up. I had to step up and help my family as quickly as I could, so I shadowed my mother as she prepared me for my first real job. She taught me how to wipe my aunt's ass after she waddled down the hallway with her walker to use the restroom. She showed me how to give her a sponge bath in the shower while she sat on a chair. I learned about each pill she took, why she took it, when she needed to take it, and whether or not she needed to take it with food. This last part was particularly important so she wouldn't get sick to her stomach—but then my mom showed me how to clean it up when she did.

We all became prisoners to a situation that took control of our household. Mom and Grandma Jane were working to pay off debt, trying to decide who would take care of what, and struggling not to fight about every decision (the way an indebted married couple might fight over how to handle the money being thrown in every direction). Teresa sunk into what looked like a deep depression, or maybe she was just doped up. She slept a lot—more than half the day usually—and I struggled with my own identity in this messed-up world where I suddenly lost my childhood. I had become an adult, and as the only person in the house who didn't work outside the house, it was now my responsibility to babysit the very person who had done the same for me.

Not all of you will relate to this, and as I write some of you might pick up on things that not even I understood—or understand now—because you're in the adult category of this situation. Or maybe you're like Teresa, the victim to it. But I was still very much the child in this situation. My life took a turn, switched tracks, and I didn't know

RAISED BY NARCOTICS—Diet Coke and Painkillers

where I was going. I still had this weird hope and belief that my life would work out anyway, because I was a child and the world was my oyster. As I grew older, though, those dreams faded, until they eventually died altogether. I can tell you the exact moment when that happened—but not right now.

Maybe you also know the exact moment your dreams died. Could you have controlled that? Could you have forced them to become reality? Could you have chosen to keep a smile on your face despite the horrors in your home? You can choose how you react, but you cannot choose your destination, so get out a piece of paper and write down those answers to yourself as honestly as you can. What was under your control and what wasn't? Realistically, what could you have done differently? I ask this because in hindsight it's so easy to feel as if you know what you could have done, but that's exactly why hindsight is a bitch, because it's in the moment that you don't actually have those immediate answers. They only shine their know-it-all faces once the moment is long over.

At the age of twelve, when my friends were becoming babysitters to their neighbors and little siblings, I became an in-home nurse to my 37-year-old crazy Aunt Teresa. I had a choice, but did I really? Would my mother have beaten the choice into me if I had refused to do it? I can't know the answer to that, although I can guess. I would have been dubbed *selfish* and *irresponsible*. They needed me, and my mother manipulated me into the only choice

I thought I had. This pattern would continue for years and years.

At the age of twelve, I lost the ability to choose my own life. At that age, could I really have done anything differently?

CHAPTER 7

Family

Family. What does that word mean to you? My family was Diane and Cody, Grandma Jane and Aunt Teresa. And me, Alyse. Five people living and breathing in the same house. Family has taken on many meanings for me over the years, but now that I'm a little older, and hopefully a little wiser, that word essentially means "trust."

Who do you trust?

In my family, blood was everything. If you shared blood, you were there for each other—end of story. No choice on the matter. The problem is that a teenage girl growing up in a weird situation will begin to question that logic. I knew my life wasn't my own—and resentment took root as a result. My family did not love and respect me, so I didn't want to be used and manipulated simply on the fact that we all shared a bloodline. Why should I be there for them? It was always all about them. Well, what about me?

I don't know how my mother grew up, but I heard some stories. She was born in 1961 and grew up in the free-love era with Aunt Teresa. Were there drugs? Absolutely. Was there sex? Well yeah, obviously, or my brother and I wouldn't be here. Were there some deadbeat dads? Of course. Was there some experimentation with alcohol, being arrested, and living freely? Yep. So, I guess some of that happiness from being so free and wild spilled over into their adult years.

Here's what happened after Teresa's accident: there were lots and lots of prescription drugs floating around in my house. But it was okay because they were legal, right?!

Have you heard of "doctor shopping?" It is what it sounds like: you find several doctors to prescribe you the same drugs, that way you have a larger supply to get high on—or sell if you want to make a buck. It wasn't long before everyone in my family was getting high, claiming some ailment or pain and "borrowing" from Teresa. Soon my other aunts and uncles got in on it. They even paid her for them. My family quickly became a drug ring.

Did Teresa have any real hope of solving her issues long-term? No, not in a family like that. Even as a teenager, when I became emotional, my mother took one of Teresa's narcotics and broke it in half to help me calm down. I remember the very first time I took one. I trusted my mother, however manipulative she was. She was my mother, after all. I loved her and needed her in a way only a child can love and need a mommy. I still feel this way, even in my thirties. I can't remember my reason for being so anxious or crying, but she was trying to help the only way she knew how. How old was I? Probably thirteen. I couldn't

RAISED BY NARCOTICS—Family

have been much older than that, and like I said, that drug ring formed quickly. Our family members caught on fast, and who knows, maybe there were some conversations or secret deals that happened when I wasn't around.

Whatever the case may be, my mother broke a Lortab in half and gave it to me with a glass of water, the way she might give me a Nyquil tablet when I had a cold. I only got half because I was younger and smaller than everyone—and she was probably afraid of killing me on accident—so better safe than sorry. The sensation hit me fast, and before I knew it, I was both loopy and sick. I can equate it now to drinking too much, but that wasn't a feeling I knew yet. This was my first time on any type of drug or alcohol, and it was my own mother who handed it to me, convincing me that I needed it. It made me sick as a dog, and I was more miserable after taking it than I would have been if I had just gone to my room and dealt with my emotions. Luckily, before I had a chance to vomit, I passed out and slept like a rock buried under a mountain. It was possibly the best sleep of my life.

It did what she was probably hoping it would: knock me out and keep me out of the way. At the time, I was an emotional teenager who needed some sleep. Mom fixed me, and so I listened and never questioned her motives. She was only looking after me, right?! It wasn't her fault that I felt so sick—and I'm damn lucky that I did, because that sick feeling made me never want to go near any of the pills that my family was so into. I could not understand their fascination with it. I just couldn't wrap my head around it. It got to a point where everyone came up with their own reason to see a doctor and get a prescription for some narcotic, and the swapping only became more complicated as everyone started owing everyone else a certain number of pills or money. This caused a lot of tension, and I became Mom's bookkeeper of sorts, keeping track of who owed what in a little purse-sized notebook that Mom kept in her drawer. She became a control freak, and she wanted to make sure that no one was ever cheating anyone else.

I could explain everyone who was involved in all of this, but it would be easier to explain who wasn't—Grandma Jane. She stayed out of it, although her biggest concern was helping Teresa cope with the pain she inevitably went through—especially on the days she couldn't get a prescription because her pills were gone too soon. I'm sure she had some words for her children who were abusing each other, although her words would fall flat.

Where did Teresa turn to cope with that pain? Alcohol and cigarettes. On a couple of occasions, she went out with her friends for what I was told was a sleepover—but as an adult now I have to assume that she was getting drunk and high on other drugs to deal with the pain. Eventually the drug ring expanded to include her girlfriend Candice. Everyone wanted in on what Teresa had.

Wasn't Teresa just so lucky?

This was my family. We had normal family things we enjoyed—movies, holidays, little vacations. I was also being raised by not just one but several drug addicts, and I didn't know any different or any better. This was my normal.

Wasn't this just how families were?

RAISED BY NARCOTICS—Family

No one stopped it, and no one said I was being abused. What I didn't know then (but what I recognize now) was that I was being emotionally abused, mainly by my mother. If I didn't fall in line with what she expected, she called me names and slapped me. We had screaming matches where I was left in tears because she tore me down with her words, making me feel worthless. At the end of every fight, I thought it was my fault. It was always my fault for making her feel bad or hurting her feelings. I hated myself. I often went back to my room, slamming the door, writing angsty poetry and listening to loud music—Godsmack and Papa Roach—and then sat crying to myself. She called me horrible, a cruel person, a terrible daughter, a bitch. How had I become all those things? I didn't mean to be like that, but I couldn't help it. We kept fighting, but what were the fights even about?! To this day I can't even remember—I just knew that I kept starting fights that I didn't mean to start. I didn't want to believe that it was my fault, but time and time again my mother had a very convincing way of showing me exactly how it was my fault. Try as I might, her logic would always prevail. She was right—somehow it was always my fault.

It was little things, like coming home from school and forgetting to say "hi" in a pleasant tone of voice. Not cleaning a certain part of the house because she had noticed it and I hadn't (or because I didn't even realize it was my responsibility). Keeping to myself too often and not interacting with the family. Not having family dinner—which almost never happened unless she randomly decided twice a year that it would, and expected me to be all excited for it even though I wasn't.

What it boiled down to is this: I had "the wrong attitude." I didn't want to be part of the family anymore. I hated the people around me. I saw what they were doing, and even if I didn't fully understand it at the time, I knew I didn't want to be there. It pushed me down further and further into teenage depression. And worst of all, it really irked Mom. She became my bully. If I thought my fifth-grade bullies were bad, Mom was a thousand times worse. I had to tiptoe around her and be very specific about how I approached her, or all hell would break loose. We once went to a movie together, and afterwards I was so immersed in the experience that I didn't want to go home and face my own reality anymore. She hated how quiet I was on the car ride home, and she blew up at me, ranting at me, telling me how awful I was—then she stopped and refused to speak to me when I fought back. She gave me the silent treatment. That was new, and it felt like it came out of nowhere. I was suddenly desperate to have her communicate with me, to understand me, to listen to me—but she wouldn't look at me or speak to me. She didn't acknowledge me anymore, and it drove me insane. That became a new tactic of hers, and she started leaving passive-aggressive notes around the house to express her disdain for her family. It was as if she had finally figured out that she could have the last word and not feel bad about it, living only with her one-sided perspective—a perspective where we were all terrible human

RAISED BY NARCOTICS—Family

beings. I wasn't the only person she treated this way, but I was the easiest target.

Mom had always had a temper for as long as I could remember, but my childhood was a good one, and Mom never treated me that way before the drugs invaded my family. At the time we were going through it, I didn't realize it was because of the drugs. I thought she was just mean. We had our good times and we had our bad times, and if I was well-behaved, the good times lasted a little longer than the bad. Like I said, this was what normal looked like to me. I never even considered that maybe I should have talked to a neighbor or a friend—but certainly not a family member. My entire family was this way, extended and all. I assumed everyone was like this. This was just what family looked like, and because I was blood, I had to give in and let them use me however they saw fit. Not even Grandma Jane stopped Mom from treating me this way. She only pulled me away a couple of times to say how sorry she was that Mom was this way. She knew what was happening, but she didn't stop it. Maybe she didn't know how. But despite that, Grandma Jane was still my saving grace. Without her I would have been homeless. Maybe that's all she wanted: to keep me close, keep me home, and keep me safe. But I wasn't really safe, was I?

Once drugs were involved, everything escalated from bad to worse, and they never got any better. Never. There was only one thing in this world that ever made it stop. You already know what that is, but no one should ever be pushed to a point of wishing it on their family.

CHAPTER 8

Cancer

To make matters worse, Mom got sick. Really sick. I have a photo of her at Christmas one year with a brace on her arm to keep her wrist straight. She thought she had carpal tunnel syndrome. She was now working with the elderly at a home for seniors with Alzheimer's. She had a good heart, deep down, and she loved helping others. She loved being a part of that world. Funny isn't it? She was a good person, loving even. She took care of the Alzheimer's patients the way she had taught me to take care of Teresa a few years earlier—lifting them from their beds to their wheelchairs, wiping their asses when they shit in the toilet, feeding them when they couldn't feed themselves, and locking them in their rooms when they had tantrums like two-year-olds. She assumed the injury to her arm was part of that job, so she wore a brace, and continued taking drugs to help her sleep and calm her down.

Mom had a bigger problem though—her neck was swollen, and it became hard for her to swallow food, and

RAISED BY NARCOTICS—Cancer

pain kept shooting up her entire arm all the way into her shoulder. That couldn't be just carpal tunnel, so she went to see a doctor and get some tests. She was scheduled to go in for a follow up, and Teresa drove her—both because Mom couldn't drive and to provide moral support. Yeah, Teresa was still driving, and let me tell you, she was not a safe driver. She was on drugs—constantly. She was not safe, and I hated it. There were a lot of times before I learned to drive when I was in the car with her thinking, "Well, this is it. This is where my life ends." I hated driving with her, but I had no choice.

While waiting for her appointment, Mom left the exam room to find a bathroom, and a nurse approached her and asked, "So, when do you start chemo?" She meant to be calm and soothing, to offer sympathy and compassion.

Mom had not been told she had cancer. The doctor had not said anything yet. Mom lost her damn mind and came home hysterical. She had cancer, she was going to die, and already she was giving up on life. Withering away into the depths of sorrow. She didn't lay it out calmly. She stormed into the house declaring it at the top of her lungs. I didn't know how I felt. I didn't want my mother to die, but I also didn't believe her.

Sometimes she was the only person I felt truly connected to. To lose her would be devastating.

But it was a lie. The cancer wasn't real—Mom wasn't going to die. The doctor came back with test results that would need further investigation. The official result was a thyroid disorder and lupus.

If you aren't familiar with it, lupus is an auto-immune disease that eats at the healthy tissues in your body until they deteriorate. Thyroid issues often come hand in hand with autoimmune diseases, so her swollen neck made sense. This diagnosis came on her birthday, adding fuel to Mom's growing fire. She was handed more prescription drugs to aid in the healing—or rather, because there is no cure for lupus, just the masking and prevention of symptoms.

Just what Mom needed...

Now she had a reason to make everyone around her pity her the way we had all pitied Teresa after her near-fatal car accident. Pity meant love—at least I assume that's what she hoped for. Attention, love, respect—it's what she craved.

So, Mom didn't have cancer—thank God—but she did have lupus. Shit. She continued to work despite this and was even working towards getting her Certified Nurse's Assistant (CNA) certificate. She and I would sit down at the kitchen table reviewing notecards for her upcoming test, which would allow her to get a promotion—or even a better job—and make more money.

And then something happened. In her job working with the elderly who were slowly losing their minds, she worked the graveyard shift more often than not, although sometimes she got away with just the night shift and came home at midnight. There was a man she worked with, and by the way she talked about him sometimes, I assume they flirted. His name was Bruce, and he drove a motorcycle. He impressed Mom, and he was nice to her, but one night he

RAISED BY NARCOTICS—Cancer

decided to take advantage of her trust. I don't know the extent of the sexual abuse, or if it led all the way to rape, but Mom came home one night acting as if it had. She didn't tell me the full details, but she did say that she had been sexually harassed.

Eventually Bruce lost his job, but not immediately, so Mom became paranoid to go back to work. She was terrified—and it was a side of Mom I had never seen before. So many things were crashing down on her all at once. First, she had to cope with a new disease, and now this, this thing I didn't really understand at all. She lost herself in it. She became a shell of the former bull-headed woman that I knew. She crumbled. The fact that she crumbled so hard, and so fast, leads me to believe that she was raped. After her attack, she was diagnosed with Post-Traumatic Stress Disorder (PTSD) by a doctor at our local clinic.

I still have a very hard time with this. That's the thing that soldiers get after facing war, killing other human beings, nearly being killed themselves, watching their comrades get blown to pieces or innocent children murdered. How could she have been diagnosed with *that* type of stress? Such severe stress that she had flashbacks that seemed like hallucinations of the event, however violent it might have been. I've been sexually harassed, smacked on the ass by my brother's friend because he thought it was funny, but it's not something I lost sleep over. I was really pissed off, but then I let it go. I can't assume that whatever she went through was like that. It must have been so much worse, right? Was she taken back to those awful moments hiding in the closet under the stairs in her youth? Did he threaten her life if she told someone? Well, she did tell someone—a lot of someones—and maybe that's why she was so panicky about going back to work. Every time she heard a motorcycle passing on the street, she had a panic attack and hid in the bathroom and tried to drown out the noise while she sobbed. I mean, it was bad. Okay, really, really bad.

When life is really bad like that, what do you do? You see a doctor. Your family is concerned for you, and doctors make you better.

She was prescribed sleeping medication, anti-anxiety pills, muscle relaxers, and antidepressants. Not all at once, of course. First, she was panicky and couldn't sleep. Then it struck her during her waking hours, so she needed a way to cope whenever she was thrown into an anxiety attack. Then she just became depressed, and when she did sleep, she claimed to have restless leg syndrome. The next step in Mom's life was to stop working. There came a day where she just didn't go back. She called in her time off, but the next day she didn't bother with any of that hassle. She just didn't get out of bed altogether.

This was the beginning of what I call Mom's "bedridden years." Mom wasn't Mom anymore.

This is where I have questions. I understand that she had lupus and a thyroid issue, and yes, those can be very hard on your mind and body. That's an incredibly stressful thing to deal with, but what effect does taking a myriad of pills have on the body?

RAISED BY NARCOTICS—Cancer

Mom was obviously making her choices, and her choices impacted everyone around her, but I really have to stress this: she wasn't given choices *by her doctors*. She was given prescriptions that she didn't question. She trusted her doctors to do right by her, and she did what they said she should do.

Before I sat down to write today, I stumbled on another social media post that stopped me cold. This time it was a story from a local news agency about a woman overcoming her own addiction that was years in the making. It was a similar story to Teresa's: she jacked up her back at an early age, already had children, and slid down the slippery slope into street drugs before she finally came out of it to marry a cop and piece her family back together and start over. It's a warm and fuzzy story, full of hope and awareness. I appreciate her courage in posting such a personal story on a platform that is bound to get a lot of traffic.

But people are cruel on the internet. Cruel, ignorant, judgmental trolls. Most of the comments posted under that article were about how she should just control herself. She made the choice to do those drugs, so she needs to deal with the consequences. I wonder if the people posting comments like that even read the story. It was long—I almost didn't read the entire thing—and read more like a novel than a news article or blog. I love reading, especially things like this, but I doubt there were many who *actually* read it. As soon as you throw up a headline, people will attack, regardless of what is written.

No one understands what leads you down these paths. All they see is an addict who should have made better choices in life. Better choices like not getting into that car accident, not getting lupus, not being sexually assaulted.

How many trolls am I going to have at the end of this?

I have to be prepared to roll with the punches or I'm going to get eaten alive.

My family made bad choices, but they were secondary choices on things so far outside of their control that I almost can't blame them for everything that happened. In all honesty, the people I blame are the ones who have the most power in the situation. Doctors are in a position to steer you in the right directions to make better choices, to give you long-term solutions, to empower you to be strong and work your way forward, not fall into the depths of the never-ending cycle of drugs and, ultimately, death. But, sadly, that is where the money is made, and money trumps all. You can't make money on success stories, because once someone is successful, they'll stop buying your product. Well, you can't make money on a dead woman either—unless you shape her life to include her young and impressionable daughter to become just like her when she grows up.

Where are my choices in life? Do I really have any when this is the only life I've ever known? My one week participating in the D.A.R.E (Drug Abuse Resistance Education) program during fifth grade is not going to be enough to combat the years of watching my family believe every word their trusted doctors told them. Those are some heavy nuances that my mind was just not ready for. No one thinks of their doctor as a drug lord, but everyone should.

CHAPTER 9

Dreaming of Death

After her accident, Aunt Teresa scared me. I hated driving with her because she was always high. She would swerve in and out of lanes to the point that I would have to occasionally pull the wheel back in the correct direction. She would say something like, "Oh," and gave an embarrassed smile. We also fought about a lot of things, like her smoking or drinking. I would snoop through her room and find bottles of alcohol, then show them to Grandma Jane who just shook her head. None of us knew what we could say or do to battle the never-ending struggle that was my crazy Aunt Teresa. I begged her to quit smoking, lecturing her (as I was lectured at school time and time again) about just how bad it was—not only for her, but for all of us, too. It wasn't just me, a child, sitting in a home full of second-hand smoke, but our two dogs and cat were also unintentionally harmed by it as well. I had strong opinions, and I shared them. Mostly Teresa would just sit there and listen, but sometimes she would fight back; other times she would walk me out to the dumpster and throw away her full carton of cigarettes to prove a point—a point that never lasted very long. We hugged, and fought, and hugged, and fought, and talked, and fought—a constant up-and-down cycle. The older I got, the more I thought I knew her—and the more I wanted to help her control everything that was going wrong in her life. Mom was controlling me, I was controlling Teresa, and we had this weird family dynamic where sometimes we got along and sometimes, we didn't. When we didn't get along, we just avoided each other, like the other person was rotting and we didn't want to smell their stink. We were kind of awful to each other.

Often, I was so sick of living in that house that I just wished everyone would die. It was pretty common for me to start imagining all the ways they could die, and suddenly become horribly afraid of it actually happening. I just wished I was free of them, and the only answer to that freedom was their death. I would imagine in my head the horrible accident that would take their lives, and then dream of what life would be like afterward, just me and Grandma Jane, peacefully living our lives—but then I would feel like an awful person and hate myself for thinking that way. I would say to myself, "No, you don't wish that, that's horrible!" I'd shake my head as if shaking the gruesome images out of my ears. More often than not, I just got stuck in my daydreams of living a different life. Everything that could come with finally becoming an adult: going to college, moving out, getting a real job, taking care of myself. I spaced out a lot, so much that my brother

RAISED BY NARCOTICS—Dreaming of Death

nicknamed me the "space cadet." Completely true, and I couldn't even fight him on it. My daydreams were my only hope of changing my reality. I needed something to hold onto, so I stayed in my own head as often as I could—sitting in my room, absorbing my music, and writing poetry in my journal.

Eventually, I turned sixteen. My sixteenth birthday was great; Mom put some good effort into throwing me a decent sweet sixteen party. We went to the family house of my new sister-in-law—Cara, Cody's wife— where they had a swimming pool in the backyard. Some quick back story on Cara: I have known her since I was maybe four years old. Maybe earlier. She's always been a big sister to me. She and Cody dated off and on since they met each other in junior high, until they eventually found each other again as adults and got married. True high school sweethearts. Swimming in her family's backyard pool became normal. Her family became our family, and I tagged along enough to be able to place her family in my comfort zone. They have always been very welcoming. That family has a special place in my heart.

So, at the sweet sixteen pool party with my family, Mom bought me a beautiful sheet cake covered in frosted roses with my name across the top. Meanwhile, Cody teased me with a card that held the keys to a car—although it just turned out to be a little Match Box PT Cruiser with flames on either side, something I kept saying I would put on my car if I ever got one.

Before and after this party, though, something happened that would ultimately change the course of my adult life.

Mom was committed. To where? I don't actually know, and yes, it happened two separate times within only weeks of each other. The first time happened just before I started Driver's Ed to get my driver's license, just a few weeks before my sweet sixteen. It was something I had been looking forward to for a VERY long time. Driving provided a new freedom that I couldn't wait to taste. This is the time that stands out in my head, but the details are hard to recall. I remember Mom and Grandma talking it over. From my perspective, it had to be on Mom's terms whether or not she went to rehab—but I don't know why I call it rehab, because to be honest, I don't know what it was. Truthfully, I don't. After everything that had gone wrong for Mom, the doctors decided that she needed to be sent to a facility of some kind to get help. I even heard the phrase "she's a danger to herself" a few times. Ultimately Mom decided it was the best thing to do. Grandma Jane drove her there, and all I could know was that it was somewhere in Salt Lake City and she would be there for a couple of weeks.

During that time, Cody decided it would be great to go visit her and show support. Of course, I tagged along. I was very curious to see Mom and hear about what was going on. However, after the long drive to SLC, we were made to wait in the waiting room just inside the entrance. Mom's entire visit had to be supervised, and it was all incredibly awkward. I don't know what Mom was feeling in that moment, but I can guess that it was shame and humiliation. That was rather transparent. Not once did she smile or look happy to see any of us. We all sat on couches facing each other—me, Cody, and Cara on one, and Mom across from us on the other, with a long glass coffee table separating us. Mom directed all of the conversation at Cody, and it seemed as if she was trying to avoid any eye contact with me whatsoever. The conversation was basic, shoot the breeze how-are-yous, short and to the point. Cody caught on pretty fast that maybe we were unwelcome guests, and he asked if we should leave. Mom simply nodded. We all stood, and my heart broke just a little bit. Mom didn't want to talk to me. She didn't want to look at me. I tried to hug her before we left, and she gently patted my back once, and then turned to hug Cody and walked back down the hall from whence she came as quickly as she could. What was wrong with my mother? I didn't know then, and I don't know now. Questions left unanswered.

Eventually she came home, and everything went back to a semi-normal. And then it happened a second time. I can't recall exactly why, but this time I had my driver's license and I was using Mom's car to drive myself around. It was the end of the summer, just before school started. I remember it happened quickly. Mom was sent there? Maybe directly from her doctor's office? The only reason I make this guess is because she didn't have anything with her when she was committed the second time. The second time I took her car and packed her suitcase with things from her bedroom. By this time we were no longer sharing a room, because Cody had moved out to start his new life with Cara and I finally got my own room—more freedom, yay! This time I had a list that Grandma Jane had written down for me, which consisted of items Mom was not allowed to have for fear that she might hurt herself with them—or potentially kill herself. No belts, no tweezers, definitely no razors, nothing chemical, etc. Just basic clothing and that was it. I drove up in the evening hoping to be there before visiting hours were over, but no one would let me see her. I handed a nurse the suitcase I had packed for Mom, and right there in the lobby she opened it up and pulled everything out to examine what I had brought with me. She was incredibly thorough, and it scared the hell out of me.

What the fuck were you doing in there, Mom?

Mom was losing her grip on reality and life. I was simply blind to everything going on around me.

These instances marked the beginning of my freedom. My freedom to drive myself where I wanted, and my freedom to start looking for a job—which meant that I could help support myself and my family that was weirdly broken.

With a little trial and error, I ended up finding a job working at the local Wendy's, one of the only fast food joints in my little city of Spanish Fork, Utah. Between the new job and my school load, I lost myself in my new reality. I was just so happy and relieved to not have to be home anymore. I started making real friends and feeling a kind of home-away-from-home vibe at my new job. The people I worked with started feeling more like family than my own family did. They cared about me. They let me talk about it,

RAISED BY NARCOTICS—Dreaming of Death

they let me cry, they let me eat there when I had nothing to eat at home. My starting wage was $6.10 per hour, and I worked part-time. It was enough to help with some groceries at home and put gas in the cars.

There's a big problem making money, though, when you're young and have a very manipulative parent. (You can see where this is going.) I wasn't doing enough for our family, and after Mom had come home from her second rehab experience and recognized that I was becoming a stable working woman, she started making lists and demanding that I get her certain things and start paying for prescriptions. She had some really compelling arguments, but they were never discussed with me on an adult level—they were just thrust into my hands as I was being told I needed to step up for our family. She said now that I was old enough, it was really about time I started contributing—even though I was already giving everything that I had.

Where I once felt proud of my earnings and my job, now I started resenting the fact that I worked. I worked so damn hard, and for what? Just to throw my own money away on more pills and useless shit they didn't need. Clothes, cigarettes, ice cream, candy bars, even nights out eating for the entire family. I mean, this shit adds up when you're making only six bucks an hour. I had no money to my name, ever. Nothing left for me at the end of the day. Cody started lecturing me on saving money and how important it was, but how was I supposed to do that when I had this weird family I was trying to take care of? I felt incredibly responsible for them, especially considering everything Mom was going through.

By then it was summer of 2003, and I was seventeen. I was excited to go off into my last year of high school. I had gained just enough credits to scoot by without going to the last half of the school day, so I started going to work full time because I hated my house and everyone in it.

By this time, it was painfully obvious that Teresa was a full-blown drug addict. We gave her a hard time for it so many times, trying to intervene and set her on the right path. It never worked. Meanwhile, Mom was losing herself in her depression and disease. Her skin was breaking out in little volcanoes all over her arms and face. She no longer dared step outside, and I thought she had become practically a zombie. She lost all willpower to so much as get out of bed every day. She just stayed in her room, or in her robe in the living room drinking coffee while watching Judge Judy. Both she and Teresa were now on some type of government assistance for their disabilities. Mom got a regular check from the Workmen's Compensation Fund because of her ordeal at her last job, as well as social security for her disease, right along with Teresa who still earned food stamps.

Grandma Jane attempted to retire somewhere in the mix of all of that, hoping to stay home and take care of her two adult children who didn't have their lives together. But she ran out of money really quick and had to go back to work. She first went to work at Walmart, where they treated her like shit. She came home two weeks later and refused to

RAISED BY NARCOTICS—Dreaming of Death

go back, but then she found work at a bookbinding factory, where she settled into a routine and made a few new friends.

What I hated most was watching Grandma Jane lose her fire for life. She was the strongest person I knew, and yet, she was crumbling under the pressures that both Mom and Teresa imposed on her. She and I worked together to provide for the family, me covering mostly just the groceries, and her paying for the second mortgage that she had to take just so we could survive (and pay off some of the terrible medical debts).

There was a routine, and for the most part we all stuck to ourselves. We interacted a bit, and Mom and Teresa eventually built this best friend-type bond because they spent their waking hours together, smoking in the living room downstairs and talking about their hardships in life. Meanwhile, I was just trying to finish school and working full time to both escape my reality at home and help out financially. Grandma Jane was working full time, coming home for a cup of coffee then just going to bed early.

Part of me feels that it's not entirely fair to sum up our lives like this. It may seem like I'm forgetting the good times, but I truly can't remember that many. There were some new babies that Cody and some of my cousins were now having after getting married, and we were able to babysit them while they figured out their work-life balance. That cheered up every single person in the house. Occasionally on Sunday afternoons (when no one else was at the theater because they were all at church), Mom would take me to see the newest Hollywood blockbuster where we would laugh and joke the whole time and come home in a really good mood. Sometimes we went shopping together, not because we needed anything, but because life was too short and meaningless, so why not have a little fun? There were the summer trips to my Grandpa Bill's house in St. George where it was always sunny and hot, and I got to go swimming for hours and live a more carefree life. It was there that Mom was always convinced that she was finally going into remission. She was happier there, and Grandpa Bill would take us out to eat, or drive us to cool landmarks where we could explore and feel happy. We never felt happier than when we were with Grandpa Bill. I very much believe that my mother's relationship with her dad was her favorite. They were best friends, even after all that time. She hated leaving him, so much so that anytime at home afterward, she was miserable. I'm positive that she might have moved in with him if he allowed it, but he lived in a little retirement community in a home that had been paid for by one of his step-children.

If there weren't any good memories mixed in with the bad, then I don't see how anyone could survive a life like that. But I still contemplated suicide on good days, and I wished I was brave enough to throw myself off the cliff where I would often drive to clear my head. I imagined my body rolling down, down, down, but I was actually more afraid of surviving the fall than I was of dying, and that ultimately stopped me from trying. If I was going to live, I was going to need to pull myself together, because I did *not* want to be anything like Teresa or my mother. People

RAISED BY NARCOTICS—Dreaming of Death

sometimes survived their attempts to end their lives, and who was going to take care of me if that happened? I needed to be sure it would work, and I just never was. I knew how worthless I was to those people, and I didn't want to end up in an even worse situation when I couldn't handle this one to begin with. I needed control of what happened to me.

Being a senior in high school, on the verge of becoming an adult, I still had hope—so I pushed forward and held onto my dreams. I chose to live instead of die, just in case I might still have something to live for.

CHAPTER 10

A Life Not Lived

I had gone to Walmart to dig through their CD bins or find a new one that I liked. I wanted to escape into the music and out of reality, something I did every day of my life. I always had music in my ears one way or another. I ended up buying the newest Sarah McLachlan CD. I opened the case in the car on the way home and popped it in, singing at the top of my lungs because I loved singing so much. I came home with the music stuck in my head, the CD case in my hand. On my way down the stairs into the second-hand smoke-filled basement, I ran into Teresa. She saw the CD and made light conversation, asking which one it was. When I showed it to her, she got excited. She said she loved Sarah McLachlan, and she asked if she could borrow it one day. I said she totally could, maybe we could listen to it together—then she made a joke that she already listened to my music every day through my closed door because my stereo was so loud. We both laughed.

RAISED BY NARCOTICS—A Life Not Lived

Somehow the conversation changed from that to how cold my feet got at night when I was sleeping, so she went to her room to get a pair of slipper socks for me to help me keep them warm. She gave me a hug and a kiss on the cheek, and we said goodnight to each other with smiles on our faces. In that moment we loved each other, we were friends, we were connecting. I'm happy to remember this moment, because it was the last conversation I would ever have with her. All the things that could have happened that night, all that could have been said or ignored, we were actually kind to each other.

Maybe that's what makes everything that followed feel like it was entirely my fault. I couldn't have known in that moment how much pain she was in. She seemed happy, so now years later I can only guess that she was on one of her many drugs, and it was working in full effect. She was feeling good, something that rarely happened for her anymore. Her body had built a tolerance to her various narcotics, and she was being prescribed a new one every so often that was more potent. It would take a larger edge off, but as time passed, she did not feel the same relief with the same doses. This was how we all knew she was an addict, and she didn't care if she was or not. She didn't want to live with her pain, so we all let her be addicted. It was so much easier than having her try something else. Something else always costs more, and we definitely were not the type of family that could afford rehab facilities of any kind.

I woke up that night to pee. That happens a lot. I have a lot of restless nights thanks to my tiny bladder, and no I don't think I have any disease or illness, because trust me I've been tested for various disorders. I think, really, I just tend to wake up to any noise whatsoever, or any sensation. This night—the very early morning of March 6, 2004, a Saturday—I believe it was two things that woke me up: my bladder and Teresa's snoring. She always snored really loudly, and we often teased her for it. My room was at the bottom of the stairs in the basement, and hers was down the hall, but we shared walls. Her room was also next to the bathroom, with a shower that didn't work and a hole in the wall that looked into the laundry room. The floors were lifting from their seams, the walls had water stains from years of use and neglect, and a small window peered into the backyard right under Grandma Jane's honeysuckle bush.

    I hated going down that dark hallway. There was no light. I was paranoid and afraid of everything. I was afraid of the dark, of all the things that lurked there that I wasn't aware of. I kept my eyes down, turning on lights as I went, making sure to keep my eyes from looking into the darkest part of the house. I passed the spooky laundry room, hauled ass down the hall to pee, then ran back to the only place I ever felt safe—my bedroom.

    On my way down the hall, I heard her snoring. I was half asleep, wishing my bladder hadn't woken me up again. It sounded a little different this time, and I did—I did— think twice about it. I sat on the toilet quickly—the same one I had taken her to many times right after her accident, to help her sit, stand, and wipe her ass—and I listened to her snore. There was a little gurgle, like she was snoring with water in her throat. But she was snoring, so that meant she was breathing. I went back to bed. I didn't think much more of it other than that. This still haunts me.

I woke up to Mom screaming at Teresa. No, not really screaming, but saying her name loudly. I walked down the hall where I saw Mom standing over her, slapping her face and yelling, "Teresa, wake up, dammit!" I stood there, dumbfounded. Teresa wasn't waking up. Mom rushed out, saw me, ran into the bathroom for a cup of water, came back out and splashed it all over Teresa's face. Still nothing. She didn't wake up. She just lay there, unmoving, still making that gurgling sound I had heard in the middle of the night, now drowning in the cup of water that Mom had splashed on her.

"I'll handle this Alyse," Mom said as she slammed the door in my face. "Just go upstairs. Grandma needs your help today."

What was I supposed to think? I didn't know how to react. Mom would handle it. Maybe Teresa was just sleeping off a heavy dose of painkiller. This had happened before, but not to this extreme. She had at least always woken up if we shook her or slapped her face.

I ran upstairs, where Grandma Jane told me she needed me to take her car into the tire shop to have her tires rotated. I got ready really quickly, grabbing at both my chance to leave the house and have alone time anywhere in the world, even a dingy car shop. I thanked Grandma Jane for just wanting to get me out of the way.

ALYSE NEIBAUR

As I sat at Big-O Tires on the east side of Main Street in Spanish Fork, I heard the sirens from the fire station a block or so down the road. Main Street was not a long stretch of road, so you could hear those sirens at any point along the street. I just happened to be able to hear them, stand up, walk to the window, and watch what direction they were going. Sure, Spanish Fork was a small city back then, but I knew without a doubt that they were headed to my house. As soon as that realization hit me, the phone rang in the shop. I watched the man at the desk answer, keeping my ears tuned at the sirens now growing distant as they raced to my address. He looked right at me. "Are you Alyse?" he asked. I nodded. I needed to go home. They were taking Teresa to the hospital. I knew all of this before I took the phone from his hands and heard Grandma Jane's voice on the other end telling me exactly that.

They finished with the car as fast as they could, and I raced home just in time to see the ambulance close its doors with Teresa inside and race away to the hospital.

Grandma Jane was with Teresa in the ambulance. Mom and I would have to drive down separately. Mom was scrambling to put herself together, yelling at me about everything that had happened while I was gone. They had tried to do CPR on her while she was in the bed, but the bed was too soft, so they had to move her to the floor, but it wasn't working. They lifted her onto the ambulance bed and whisked her away. Mom said she knew Teresa was already gone. There was no oxygen going to her brain—she was probably brain dead. No one had told her this, she had come to her own conclusions after watching elderly people exit the world in the same painful manner at the Alzheimer's center. Mom called the sound Teresa had been making the "death rattle."

And when she said that, my world stopped.

I kept it all to myself—the fact that I had woken up and heard her making that new noise. That I just chalked it up to snoring. I blamed myself for not waking anyone up to come see what was going on. I never told anyone. I held it in and blamed myself for what came next.

We sat in the hospital for three-and-a-half days before they "pulled the plug" on Teresa's oxygen, the only thing keeping her alive. As her organs shut down one by one, doctors came into the waiting room to gently explain what was happening and how Teresa would never come home again. They told us she had had a stroke, but later we discovered that her stroke was caused by the very thing she had relied on all of these years to keep herself alive and out of pain—her narcotic painkillers. Specifically, it was a new patch that slowly released the drugs through the pores of the skin. She had put one on during the day, and in an effort to relieve her pain enough for her to sleep through the night, she put a second one on her other arm. Now she would sleep forever.

It was all to control her pain, the searing pain that most of us have no concept of because we've never experienced it. We spent three days of turmoil watching Teresa's lifeless form in the ICU, her mouth hanging open with tubes protruding from it, cords hanging around her body, and a constant beeping that told us her heart was beating, but she wasn't really there. Zero brain activity, even though her heart still pumped blood and her lungs still pulled in oxygen. Three days watching my family make decisions, Uncle Karl stepping in as her big brother (as if he had any authority on the matter) and bringing in his own doctor. My aunt Sylvia, Teresa's youngest sister, sitting quietly next to me watching everyone have a say while her sister slowly drifted from life. Me wondering, what now? I came and went from the house until the decision to pull the plug was finally made early Tuesday morning.

    I stood by my mother, who grabbed for my hand and gave me a weak smile. We stood together, united in grief over what was happening. She squeezed my hand in fear, holding onto me as if I possessed all of the strength in the room, and she needed it to survive this moment. Grandma Jane sitting by Teresa's left shoulder, stroking her oldest daughter's hair as the life left her face and lips. Uncle Karl on Teresa's other side, hovering over her body until her lips started turning blue, then flinging himself on top of her, sobbing like a baby and screaming her name as if they had been best friends for all of these years, despite the judgment that he and his family had heaped on her for being a sinner. Sylvia sitting quietly by the wall watching Karl's theatrics along with the rest of us. Tears running down all of our faces.

    I couldn't handle staying to watch the life drift out of Teresa. Mom was incredibly understanding when I whispered to her that I would meet her at home. I gave her a hug and slowly walked out of the room.

This was my first experience with death, and I wasn't sure how to cope with it. The way I had taught myself to cope with stress after all these years was to be alone. To get in the car and drive somewhere. Mom panicked a little when she tried calling the house phone and I hadn't been there to answer. I had gone to this place we Spanish Fork hicks knew as The River Bottoms. It was on River Bottoms Road, meandering through the streets at the base of the mountain. There was a place you could climb to, a cliff just below the mountainside homes, with an incredible view of the valley. This was the cliff where I had sat countless times, contemplating my life and how I could end it—the cliff I came to, yet again, to ponder what it was truly like to die. Teresa was doing just that, dying. Maybe she was already gone. Maybe if I had stayed even two minutes longer I would have witnessed the life leaving her body. What I needed though was air. I needed to breathe fresh air into my lungs to cope with the tragedy hitting my family, and all that meant for me and my existence in it.

CHAPTER 11

Touching the Dead

We held Teresa's funeral three days after she passed away. Before the ceremony, Teresa was dressed and lying on a flat table, and she looked more like a wax figure than a human being. I had never been that close to a dead person before, but she was *my* dead person, so I felt privileged to touch her skin, however fake it seemed. I had not expected her to feel as rock hard as she did. Her skin was leathery, much like the pet iguana Cody had brought home when I was five.

Mom was heating up her curling iron on a chair next to Teresa. Her hands shook as she plugged it into the wall, and she began fumbling with the contents of her makeup bag—not Teresa's, because Teresa had never owned enough to justify an entire bag. I never understood why Teresa ever wore makeup, however rare it was—it just didn't suit her. She wasn't a typical woman, but here she was, dressed in that same green floral dress that she wore to every event—wedding, baptism, or funeral—and Mom was trying to pull

RAISED BY NARCOTICS—Touching the Dead

herself together enough so she could apply that final coat of foundation and mascara and fluff up Teresa's hair for her final goodbye.

At first, I was scared to walk into the funeral home with Mom and help her with this task. Dead people were somehow intimidating, and every environment became more and more unfriendly: the ICU, where she took her last breath; the cold and sterile room with machines humming a low tone or beeping in the background; now the funeral home that was meant to feel comforting, like someone's living room, with warm colors and flowers placed on a handful of surfaces to seem inviting. It was far from inviting, though. It felt old and musty, more like a haunted house.

I was so curious about Teresa and how her skin felt now that she was dead that I hadn't yet registered my own emotions. I think it threw Mom off what she was trying to accomplish. She kept darting her eyes up at me as we both hovered over Teresa, Mom attempting to apply the foundation that stubbornly wouldn't adhere to her skin because she was no longer porous, and me running my fingers over her carefully placed hands that rested across her belly. Growing up, I had wanted to become an archaeologist, study the long-dead. They were fascinating to me, and had such stories to tell—but what I really wanted was to work with their bones, and Teresa was far from being just bones and decaying muscle. She was still too human, and it creeped me out. I knew I could never deal with freshly dead people—that was gross—but if they had been dead for a long time, that would have been my dream come true. I wondered silently to myself how long it would take Teresa to become bones. Now that the embalming fluid ran through her body, would she ever?

At that moment, Mom became impatient with me.

"Alyse, just go. I should just do this alone."

She said it so quickly and forcefully that all my emotion registered at once as I jumped at her words. I walked out as fast as I could, the tears finally starting to well up and spill over. I found a table in a side room that had a box of tissues sitting on it, with a bench perfectly placed just for the off chance that you might need somewhere to sit while you cried. It just so happened that I did, and once the tears started flowing, I couldn't make them stop. I sobbed long and hard into those tissues, as quietly as I could, throwing them away one by one into the trash—also conveniently placed to the side of the table.

Her funeral felt both awkward and devastating. I had been given two jobs in preparation for it: creating a slideshow and reading a poem. For the slideshow, I selfishly picked photos that displayed me with her, although as I stood watching the slideshow at her funeral, I quickly realized how big of a mistake that had been. And it had been another mistake picking her favorite song by Evanescence and hearing it loop over and over again, ruining that song forever. I would never be able to hear any song by that band without the flashback to this major event in our lives.

My second job was to write a poem in her honor to recite at the church. This had been my idea, but again, as I

RAISED BY NARCOTICS—Touching the Dead

stood from my seat to start walking to the dais, I realized what a mistake I had made in volunteering myself to say anything at all, let alone recite poetry. I was hardly eloquent.

At the end, before they closed her casket forever, we all stood in a long line and said one last goodbye, while some of us placed items around her to be held inside with her like a time capsule. The dreaming archaeologist in me wondered if anyone would ever open her casket to find these items and try to analyze them to better understand our long-lost culture. I put my poem and a letter I had written to her next to her hands. In doing so, I realized she would never read them. She would never know or understand how much I had loved her, while simultaneously hating her. I felt more guilt than I could ever put into words for not saving her life when I had the chance.

That was the second moment that changed our lives forever. A moment we had no control over. A moment in which I lost my dreams, and myself.

Teresa was my aunt—not my mother, not my sister, and most times not even my friend. Just an extended family member that I had grown up with, and shared a birthday with year after year. But she was more than that. She was a person I took comfort in when I was child as she hugged me in a way no one else ever would. She loved me so unconditionally, like her own child. But it took her death for me to truly and finally open my eyes to it. She was a person I nursed and cared for at a young age when she needed that same unconditional love from someone who wasn't going to pass judgment when she was at her most vulnerable.

Maybe I failed her in those moments of her life. Maybe she was forever grateful. We never talked about it. To me, she was the sister I never had—both annoying and incredibly protective. She was the person who started the mess of a life that I lived in. The person who helped me realize my dreams; the person who took them to her grave with her when she died.

Who was Teresa? She was everything that I never realized I needed in another human being until she was gone. In her death, I broke. Fully and completely. I do not remember most of the days that came afterwards, but what I do remember is a strength I didn't know I possessed in the sudden and sharp realization that this was not the life I wanted for myself. I could not and would not let myself crumble. I was going to be someone different, even if that meant living in reality instead of the made-up world of hopes and dreams I had survived in for all of those years. But reality isn't an easy place to live in.

CHAPTER 12

My Own Drugs

Somehow, miraculously, I graduated high school, and in doing so I quickly realized that my adult life was going nowhere. I say miraculously because once Teresa died, so too did my desire to do much of anything. I believe that my teachers took great pity on me and let me slide considering how close to graduation I was. There were certain days near the end that I just couldn't tolerate sitting in class. The school counselor had told me that I could come sit in her office if I became too overwhelmed, and I took her up on it. Even though she tried to get me to open up about my feelings, mostly I just sat quietly waiting for the bell to ring for my next class.

I was about to turn eighteen, and I would then have the freedom to do as I pleased. If that meant getting into my car and driving until I ran out of gas, then I could. Maybe I should have. That idea scared me and invigorated me at the same time. Mostly, though, I found myself depressed. Why? Because my family was literally falling apart, one insignificant life at a time, and all my dreams had been buried with the woman who started the downward spiral that was my life.

I was working full time, but I started having panic attacks on the job. The normal rush of people coming and going from our little fast food joint at the bottom of the mountain was stressing me out so badly that I lost control. I had to hide in the manager's office and cry to myself, trying to pull myself together. I couldn't handle life anymore. We had all been through so much, and through all of it I held onto this hope that somehow, someday, it would get better. I mean, it had to—right? But now, one of us was dead, and I realized that with that death, there had never been any hope. I could look back and see how stupid I was for thinking that my life could be any different. My friends at work were getting excited for college, planning their lives, while I would very likely be stuck working there for the rest of my life. I would never even be close to average. I would always fall below the line, and now that Teresa was dead, I had to change it—or end it.

I was cutting myself. I was smoking. I didn't care. Mom and Grandma Jane didn't care. I was becoming one of them. I sat in the basement with them—but not in Teresa's spot, no one would ever sit there again. It would sit as a reminder of what we lost. No, I sat in the Lazy Boy next to Grandma Jane, who was in her normal seat by the fireplace, Mom sitting next to her in her pajamas, the only thing she would wear anymore. And we all smoked together.

RAISED BY NARCOTICS—My Own Drugs

In my despair, I found the courage to ask Mom to take me to the clinic to see a doctor about what was happening to me. I knew I needed to do something about my depression, my new anxiety at work, and the fact that I was using physical pain as a release from the emotional pain. When we arrived at the clinic, I tried to explain myself, but it was hard. Mom was sitting next to me, and she had an annoyed look on her face as she said, "Well, I'm not going to tell them. You have to do it." I was ashamed of myself for being so weak. She told me all the time that I just needed to deal with it, to suck it up. Why did I ask her to bring me? Was I still looking for support from her? I was never going to get it. I wanted her to see what I was going through, but I realized that she didn't care. I was just like her now, sitting in a doctor's office, asking for drugs to ease the pain of my daily life. It was a choice I was making, because it was either this or die. It felt like my last resort, and I was so confused. I was lost. I felt alone, and not alone. I wished I was truly alone. I couldn't escape her, yet I desperately wanted her to see me.

"I think I'm depressed," I said quietly, embarrassed at how the doctor was looking at me. The muscles in my legs started to shake. I was seventeen, and thought I had depression. I wasn't sure, and I needed someone to tell me why I felt this way—or what I needed to cope with it.

Teresa was dead. My life had been a living hell. I was only now starting to piece together that I had been emotionally abused for years, but I was so ashamed. It felt like it had been a mistake to come here, to open up. I couldn't *truly* open up, because she was sitting right there, watching me, judging me, and whatever I said here would come home to haunt me.

"I've been cutting myself," I said, even quieter. The doctor looked at my ankle as I uncovered the scars and fresh wounds I had inflicted upon myself. He looked disgusted by me. He seemed impatient. What was I supposed to say? He didn't ask me why I did it. He had heard enough. I thought I had depression and I was cutting myself, and here my mother sat looking normal enough. She had put makeup on and gotten dressed, and yelled at me to leave her alone because it was my fault she had anxiety about leaving the house in the first place. But the doctor hadn't seen what happened before we left, or what would happen when we got home. What he saw was a depressed teenaged girl, who hadn't said anything about her dead aunt, or the pains of life over the course of her entire adolescence. He saw a girl who cut herself for attention. He saw an exhausted mother who was not sure how to cope with such a dramatic teenaged girl who was just seeking attention.

He prescribed me an antidepressant called Cymbalta, something he said was less powerful than other drugs like Zoloft. He hadn't believed me. My heart was pounding so fast. This felt like such an awful mistake. I needed to get out of there. I took the paper and we left. I took Mom home, because she'd had enough, and then I took my piece of paper and my purse to fill my very own prescription, repeating the cycle of drugs I had watched my family fall

RAISED BY NARCOTICS—My Own Drugs

into over the last six years. Then I drove to my spot on the cliff-side to contemplate the reasons I would either jump this time, or cave to the drugs that seemed like my only option in dealing with a life I couldn't face anymore.

CHAPTER 13

Too Fat

Family patterns are real. When you grow up in a family of devout religious folk, you'll likely follow that pattern. Suppose you grow up in a family raised on a farm in the country, mostly self-sustained, and you'll likely find comfort in having a lot of land, growing your own food, and raising animals. Family pattern. Comfort zone. You live what you know. I've heard of people in the Bronx growing up only knowing drugs and violence, and then when someone takes them away and finally says to them, "This isn't okay," they respond with, "I didn't know."

All you can know is how you are raised. We all live inside a very small box. Our view to the outside world incredibly limited. Social media and technology may have changed that a bit, but let's swing back to the 90s and early 2000s, when I bought my very first flip-phone that could also take photos. That damn thing cost so much money.

We didn't have then what we have now. Most Millennials forget this. This technology, this connectivity has only been around since I was twenty-something. What would my life back then have been like if I had the ability to rant about it on Facebook? What if I could live stream the mess of my family on YouTube? What could have been different if I had the chance to set up a GoFundMe page for my Aunt Teresa? Would she have been able to get the physical therapy she should have?

What I had was a problem: where was my life going? I knew I didn't want to be like them—my aunt who died of a drug overdose, my Grandma Jane who had to work full-time in her sixties and still not meet the needs of her adult children living with her, and my Mom with her lupus and PTSD that was slowly killing her.

I had to do something. I still had options. But I had to put on my big girl pants and realize that college—the ultimate dream, the thing everyone told you that you needed to be successful—was not an option for me. Not with my history, not with my family patterns in the way. Sometimes, unless someone is standing in front of you, pointing out the ways it can still be done, you just can't see it. Not to mention how much self-discipline I would have needed to overcome everything I was going through.

So, if it wasn't college, what was my next step? One day Mom pulled me aside with an idea. It seemed like something that she had been planning to talk to me about for a while, a way to get me free education and out of her hair—the Army.

The Army is not a bad choice for some people, and I did entertain the idea, so much so that I ended up at a recruiter's office. I was even assigned dates to start basic training. When they know you're curious enough to walk into their offices, they stop asking questions and just set you up to do it. I was in, done, no more outs—except for one.

Mom was excited, and I'll never know what was more appealing to her: having a kid in the military to be proud of, having me gone out of the house, or having me get a real education without dropping money on it. That hardly mattered—she was happy for me to do something meaningful for the first time in my life. I ate it up. I would do it. Sign me up, give me your papers. Basic training started in September, and I had just turned eighteen in July. It was happening.

Now all I needed to do was stand on a scale for the entrance medical exam. 192 pounds. I was 5 feet 5 inches tall and 192 pounds. I was fat. Well, duh. You could see that I was fat just by looking at me. I mean, come on. Do you really see my fat ass running courses in basic training? I'd hated my jiggly arms and enormous thighs the entire time I was growing up. I have memories of being in second grade—second fucking grade—lifting my feet off the floor while I sat at my desk and resting my heels against the legs of my chair so that my thighs wouldn't smoosh down on my seat and make me look fatter.

I don't know what Mom thought. I don't know what the recruiter was thinking when he came to our house previously and gave me all of my paperwork to ship out on my new military career. But I was told then and there, while I stood behind a thin curtain (the only thing keeping me

RAISED BY NARCOTICS—Too Fat

separated from Mom, who was waiting in a chair a few feet away), that I needed to lose weight before they could officially accept me into the military. They did not specify how much—maybe they did in terms of BMI, but I hardly remember. They probably knew that I was never coming back, although I did try. Mom encouraged me, but she got really disappointed and started looking for new options. At least she was doing something for me. In the meantime, I woke up at the ass-crack of dawn one morning, put on my sweatpants, grabbed a bottle of water, got in the car and headed to The River Bottoms to "run."

The only time I had ever run was during gym class—mostly I walked as fast as I could—and I wanted to die. I hated running, but it was the only free way to lose weight. I had no money for a gym or equipment, so me and my 192 pounds of fat hit the road.

I was too aggressive. I thought I knew the distance I was going, and this was long before Fitbit or Apple watches. All I had ever done was drive these roads, never walked them. I had no idea how far I went. I've since gone back to measure it, which turns out to be about eight miles, but that distance at that time in my life nearly killed me. I most definitely came home with heat stroke, and decided never to do it again.

For the first time in my life, I was happy being fat. So long as I was fat, the military didn't want me—and if I couldn't do this, then there was no way I would survive basic training. Truth be told, I simply didn't know what I was doing. Who was going to be my personal trainer and teach me how to run? How to lose weight? How to have the motivation and discipline necessary to be successful? I never even touched fruits or vegetables. Obviously, no one really expected me to rise to the occasion, and I didn't.

On to Plan B.

Job Corps.

Job Corps, if you don't already know, is a government-funded program that offers free education to people 16-24 years old. Sounds fancy! Also, perhaps, too good to be true?

So, I went to Job Corps. I remembered going to a Career Fair during the last stretch of my high school days, and they had a little booth set up in the cafeteria, surrounded by colleges, trade programs, or universities. You know, options for normal people. Their ads made it look like you got a cool dorm room with awesome roommates and live the college life, just like normal college kids. It sounded magical. I wanted exactly that. How awesome to be poor and qualify for this free education in some awesome areas like culinary arts or business. I qualified instantly. There were even some campuses located in Hawai'i, how awesome! Of course, you had to live in Hawai'i to qualify for Hawai'i.

As my luck would have it, there happened to be one within spitting distance of my house. Okay, maybe not spitting distance, but about a ninety-minute drive, just north of Salt Lake City in a little town called Clearfield.

All I can say is that I hope this program is doing someone some amount of good. There are kids who go there and are very serious about what they are doing, and these people manage to come out of it with a skill to go into the real

RAISED BY NARCOTICS—Too Fat

world. Even I was able to come out of it with something. At least I had that much. But it's a piece of my history that I've tried to erase in all ways possible. It could probably be its own separate book, blowing open what that institution is really all about. I may as well have been a criminal who'd been sent to prison. Because that's what it was—a fucking prison.

I'm not even sure how to sum up the six months of my life there. It was hell. I thought living at home was hell, but this place made me miss home. I missed my mom. I missed our mess—at least it was *my* mess, and I cried for days when I realized what I was doing to myself.

The Job Corps campus was a refurbished military base (hey, look Mom, you sent me to the military after all). The "dorms" were old military rooms. On the west side were the ladies, on the east side were the men, separated by an outdoor common area that was all cement and a few covered pavilions. Upon arrival we were assigned a room along a big hallway, with rooms on either side spanning the length of the hall. There were bathrooms in the middle with a few showers (which were hardly private) and one bathtub. In our rooms we were given a "closet" that was a glorified locker, maybe half again as wide as a high school locker. That's where we kept all our belongings, behind a little padlock with a combination you better hope no one gets ahold of, or your shit is gone. I brought very little with me and came home with even less. On my very first day, taking a shower and crying to myself, I left my clothes sitting outside of the shower curtain, not even second guessing my decision to leave them there while I cleaned myself off—but when I came out, they were gone. I very quickly had to change the way I handled my possessions.

That was the second lesson I learned on my first day there. The first one I learned was that there were 3,000 men to some 300 women on campus. Women were a commodity. The men, or I should call them boys, called us all "Fresh Meat." I heard that more times on my first day than I can even count. The sexual harassment began day one. By day two, I had been claimed. It is incredible what you get used to in such a short time. Mind you, I was never raped, but that doesn't mean that no one was. Sex was easy and loose, and everyone was doing it, myself included. Once I cleared my head from my confusion, I settled into my new life. I broke up with one "boyfriend," found another one, and the old one started harassing me. As I was being harassed by him, I was being lavished with attention by any other man that wanted to get laid. They just had to be a shoulder to cry on, and they knew it. It was all a sick game. How anyone actually got an education there I have no idea.

On top of that atmosphere, we couldn't leave the campus freely. We had to earn that right by means of good behavior, and we had to earn the right to our very own room in what was called "The Hotel." You started at the bottom and worked your way up. Once there, you were given a little freedom to come and go from campus. I never made it there. I was stuck, living on campus like a prisoner. I was a goddamn adult, age eighteen, and Mom had

RAISED BY NARCOTICS—Too Fat

basically thrown me in prison. I couldn't even so much as cross the street. This is how I said hello to my adult years.

The third thing I learned in a very short time was that most people were there because it was their last option—because they *were* criminals. It was that or jail, and they obviously chose that. I was almost literally inside prison gates. Maybe now you see why I want to write a second book.

Six months of my life I wasted there, and only one person ever said anything that would stick with me all of these years later. It was that first boyfriend I had there, and he said it when I cried to him about how miserable I was after only just arriving. He said to me, "This will only be a tiny dot compared to the rest of your life." I can only guess that's what he had to tell himself to get through it, too. We ended up friends in the end, and even though it was a living nightmare from beginning to bitter end, it taught me some life lessons I would never have learned otherwise, and one of those lessons is what a community looks like.

However good or bad it was, the other "inmates" there had become my family, almost in the same twisted way my own family was my family. I had a community that I relied on for comfort, support, and reassurance. We all gave each other nicknames. I had friends I only knew by those names, and they were ridiculous, like Spider, Jesus (he looked like Jesus, obviously), and Fang. I tried not having a nickname; nicknames were mostly just for the guys. I wanted to go by my real name because otherwise I was just called Bitch or Slut. You grow a thick skin after a while. First you cry and break down, then it becomes what it is, and you deal with it. But despite all the drama and heartbreak, I trusted some of them with my life. They had my back, and I had theirs.

Basically, I learned that we were all in prison together, and there was nothing to entertain ourselves after 3 p.m. each day. We were not leading normal lives where we could go to work after class or go home to watch too much TV or play video games. We couldn't head down the street to the local skate park, or gas station. What can you do in a situation like that?

First, you smoke a lot of cigarettes in a day, then you might sneak off to have sex in the bushes (yes, I did that; yes, I got caught). Then, and this is the most important part, you do drugs because what other escape do you really have? You do not live in a world like that without some form of peer pressure, and it is constant. I stuck to good old Mary Jane, but my friends did LSD, heroin, crack, and—you guessed it—pain killers.

Now, how the hell do people in Job Corps get their hands on *any* of it? Where does it come from? Who's handing it to whom?

There is a chain of people who know people who know people, extending all the way from the staff you might be friendly with, to the people with enough "good behavior" to reside in The Hotel and have more freedom to come and go from campus. We were all given a "living wage" of $32.00 every two weeks. We had an on-campus store, where I bought a winter coat—because standing outside all day in winter is brutal—and snacks and other assorted items you

RAISED BY NARCOTICS—Too Fat

might need, but its stock was very limited. Most people did not spend their money there. We spent our money on cigarettes and drugs. There were dealers, who had dealers, who had dealers.

We were bored. We were miserable. We needed escape from our lives that felt like they were going nowhere, and we had this community who helped it all feel justified. We all did it together, so it was all normal. Sure, kids were busted occasionally, and some got kicked out, but it didn't stop it. I bet if I went back and talked to some of the people there now, not much has changed at all.

I spent six months of my life there, a dot compared to the rest of my life. I'm only thirty-two, but I already can see places like downtown Salt Lake City, or "the block" as it's now being referred to, where housewives, doctors, and bums alike collect on the streets to socialize as a community and find their escape through drugs—or profit from it, or both. I understand how and why this happens. I don't hear these stories on the news and ask the ignorant question, "How could that happen?" because I get it. Unfortunately, places like that become less about the people and more about the problem. We stop seeing them as human and only see them as animals spreading a disease.

* * *

At eighteen years old, I had lived in a family of drug addicts, although I wouldn't have said it out loud at that point because I didn't see it properly—it was just my normal. I had been sent to live in a community that was one step away from prison, where people were still people but had made choices to better face their demons. And after all of that, I had finally come back home and opened my eyes to the truth of everything I had lived through, and had yet to live through. I sat, about to turn nineteen—a year after Teresa's death—on the back patio with a cigarette in my hand, watching the smoke from my exhales drift up to the stars, realizing that I was finally an adult. I truly did have my freedom now, and it was time to execute some different decisions so that I could finally live my life, instead of living the lives of those around me.

CHAPTER 14

Why Your Decisions Don't Matter

I'm a rich girl now, living in a rich family, and now the system usually works *for* me. I don't even have to sell this book and I'm set for life because of who I married and the generosity of my in-laws. Thank you, Ray and Jo. Without you, this shit isn't possible. Maybe I would be writing this from a much different perspective, but I appreciate the ability to see life from both extremes and piece together that neither extreme solves every problem.

Let's go back in time again.

I think it's safe to say that as I celebrated another summer birthday and turned nineteen, I was no closer to figuring out who I was. In fact, I went back to my job at the Wendy's drive-thru and started experiencing even stronger panic attacks than before. An entire year of my life had been wasted just for me to find myself standing in the exact same place I was before I left. That's when I decided to erase Job Corps from my life and try to forget it had even happened.

Before I left, I gave my car to Aunt Sylvia. It was the car I had taken from Aunt Teresa after she passed away, paying off her title loan (by getting another loan, what my mother called "robbing Peter to pay Paul") and using that as my transportation. It was a good car. Old, but in great condition. Dammit, I should have kept that car. I came back and had to scrounge together $200 to buy a piece-of-shit Nissan from Cody's friend, Curt, and it was constantly breaking down. I couldn't get from point A to point B without stopping, opening up the hood, letting it cool down, and either spraying some starter fluid in the carburetor or pouring gas into the tank because the fuel gage didn't work. Then I'd have to turn the key over and over again, pumping the gas pedal until the spark lit the engine and I could continue on my way.

I needed my own car, and securing one would become an important process. I could not rely on Mom's flighty feelings toward me and whether or not she felt I was suitable enough to drive her car. The very same car she hardly touched because she was now bedridden, probably going to die any day, and had lost everything she had ever held dear to her. As I heard her say these things, I would roll my eyes at her, as teenagers often do, because Mom was melodramatic on the best of days—and those were all her words. I felt bad for her, but at the same time it was hard to feel bad for her.

During this time, my cousin Mandy was in beauty school in Provo, where she also lived. Her life was coming together neatly. She had direction even though she had

RAISED BY NARCOTICS—Why Your Decisions Don't Matter

struggled just as I had (in different ways), but she was making smart decisions. Handling her money, taking care of what she had, researching the car she had purchased—not letting the engine blow up on her and being out $2,000 that she still owed to Mike down at the loan center on Main Street. No, that was me. Mandy was smarter than me. She adamantly refused to touch drugs, alcohol, or cigarettes. She pushed hard against the life we grew up in and got herself the fuck out of there, got married at eighteen (right before we both celebrated our summer birthdays), and moved out of Aunt Sylvia's apartment and into her own. She had a life of her own now, and somehow, we became disconnected. But despite that, she still managed to persuade me that doing hair was so much fun, and I should have done that with her instead of going off to Job Corps and losing myself. She hated who I was becoming, and she was not afraid to tell me about it.

Mandy, I dedicate this chapter to you and how you forced me to change, to stop going down those scary roads that were all too easy to follow.

Mandy was the support I needed to slap myself in the face, wake up, and make real changes. Changes that mattered. If she could do it, I could do it—but damn, it was going to be hard. My decisions were to:

Go to hair school just like her.

Find a reliable car so that I could get to the new school I was hoping to attend.

Search in the newspaper for a new job (yeah that was still a thing) so I could make enough money to pay for my car, car insurance, my beauty school tuition (at the time it was $10,000—now it's over $20,000. Holy sweet Jesus, can you say inflation! We're not getting a fucking degree here!), basic needs like food, and very last but not least . . .

Find shelter, or rather, my own apartment, maybe even close to the school so I could walk if I had car trouble.

So, how was I going to figure this out? I started with a school loan. First, I needed a co-signer because I couldn't pay in cash and they didn't trust me without one. That problem put damn near everything at a standstill. I couldn't think of a single person who could help. Mom, of course, had less then no credit. Same with Grandma and Aunt Sylvia, and there was no chance in hell I would ask my Uncle Karl for help. Potentially Grandpa Bill might have been able or willing to help me, but what was really standing in my way was my own pride, and quite honestly my anger at my family for not being what I needed them to be to help me get a leg up in this world. It was ultimately Cody who stepped forward and offered to help me figure out my life. He put his name on that stupid paper with me when no one else could. Somehow, with my amazing brother standing behind me, I got into beauty school. That was June 2005, just before I turned nineteen.

My next step was a new job and a new car. I worked on both in my downtime, occasionally borrowing Grandma Jane's car to get through the first ten weeks of orientation. In the next few weeks, I would go through a couple of different jobs, including one where my literal title was "Box Pusher," but I ended up getting fired because of, what?! I

RAISED BY NARCOTICS—Why Your Decisions Don't Matter

don't know. Somehow, I was not qualified to push boxes. Thank God, that job was awful.

A new car and better job happened at about the same time. I found a job where they would pay me $9.00 an hour—if I could get through training. The job was customer service support in a call center for the United States Postal Service, and because it was farther away than cosmetology school, finding a reliable car was top priority. I was finally starting to get my ducks in a row.

But dealership after dealership would not let me walk away with a car without having a co-signer, and I had no one I could ask. I couldn't muster up the courage to ask Cody again when he had already done something as huge as co-signing my student loan. There had to be a way to get a car without one. How did other people do this? I kept asking myself this question, because it felt impossible.

Finally, I found a dealership who had some pity on my situation—though at first, they almost sent me out the door empty-handed—and hooked me up with an older Hyundai Sonata. I signed all the papers, feeling pretty good about myself for checking off another box on my list so quickly, and after driving off the lot the check engine light came on, my brakes went out, and I slid into someone stopped at a stop sign. They refused to take the car back, and only fixed my brakes as a "courtesy" after lecturing me on their policy and my contract, making me feel like a complete idiot. The car still ran, so I had to go with it. Those asshats gave me a lemon. Despite my frustration, I had to keep moving forward. I was slowly starting to make it.

Just keep swimming.

Now it was time to look for an apartment but, again, without a co-signer, a deposit, and three months' income from a job, I was stuck. No matter how shitty the apartments were, I didn't qualify.

How the hell did people do this?

I wasn't homeless, thank goodness, and I always had the option of falling back into my old routine at Wendy's with the family I had grown there, but they didn't pay me enough—and I needed to move up, not down.

This all makes me think of one thing: if I couldn't get ahead, how would a homeless addict get their shit together?

My worst vice was smoking cigarettes and my situation was living with an abusive mother who kept trying to kick me out onto the streets. Now my situation was feeling dire because I was an adult, and if she meant it, then I really had to go. I would be homeless. I was one bad day from living in my Hyundai. I was starting to get desperate.

I was so damn close to making it on my own. I just needed a little more time to save the few hundred dollars necessary to put a real deposit on an apartment.

On August 8, 2005, I started my new job at the call center, training to be a customer service rep for the United States Postal Service. I had my piece of shit Hyundai Sonata that was working fine for now, even though the hood was bubbled up after the accident I had on the first day I owned it. My bank account was not really growing, but I knew with enough time and patience maybe it would. I still had debt—I could not escape it—but I was prioritizing it now and

RAISED BY NARCOTICS—Why Your Decisions Don't Matter

trying to dig myself out while simultaneously helping out with groceries at home.

Then he walked into my workplace, the nerd who was late to training because of a college class he was taking, and I thought to myself, "I would never date a guy like that." Not because he was late, but because he was a nerd, and I was into the bad-boy type. Not that that had gotten me anywhere, but I tended to size men up on first glance, and at first glance he didn't do it for me.

The only open chair was across from me. It was about to be the lucky day I had been looking for. What I would later learn is that he was also trying to break out of his shell, be more outgoing, meet women, and possibly get laid. His name was Shawn, and I wasn't his type either. The cute blonde in the class was who he set his sights on, and I saw it. So, when he started talking to me, it was out of friendship, not interest. Neither of us was interested in the other, and maybe that's exactly what we both needed. A friend. He was easily the nicest guy I had ever met. He didn't judge me for anything, didn't ask me for anything. I had never met a man like him before. We found common ground after a few short conversations, and we swapped phone numbers. I can't remember why—he was just a nice guy, and I guess I was just a nice girl. Before I knew it, as my life continued to fall apart around me, I started leaning on him for attention and eventually asked him if he would like to go out with me. I asked him as I stood bored in an electronics shop having a new stereo put into my car, something I shouldn't have been spending my money on, but music kept me sane, so it felt like a worthwhile purchase. As I meandered the store, I decided to text him. I was flirtatious because I loved the attention he gave me, and I went for the next logical step: making him mine.

This was a major turning point in my life. I would love to say, "and the rest is history," but it wasn't. We had our first date on September 11, 2005, and I remember this because the flags on our way back to my house were at half-mast and I couldn't figure out why. He pointed it out, and we laughed a little while we cried a little inside, happy now at least to have something better to remember on such a day other than the tragedy of our nation. The chemistry between us was immediate and we were engaged by October. I met his family, he met mine, and I learned very quickly how rich he was and how generous his family was. Everything was a whirlwind.

My first clue that he had money was that he had a car. Never before had I dated a man with a car. Never before had I actually dated a man, honestly. I had a handful of boyfriends (one in high school who was with me to cover up that he was gay), and a few people I had sex with, but never before had I been picked up by a man driving his very own car. Shawn was my very first look at what a normal life was supposed to look like.

After a few dates, he drove me up to his parents' house to play pool in their basement game-room. He had been excited after I told him about the pool skills I had developed in Job Corps. I remember walking into this huge home, which was apparently a downsize from their previous home

RAISED BY NARCOTICS—Why Your Decisions Don't Matter

that had included a swimming pool and carriage house. It was beyond impressive, and incredibly intimidating. The ceilings went on for miles, they had huge portraits of themselves hanging in their foyer (they had a foyer). They had a grand piano just in front of the massive wall that was a literal library of books, something straight out of *Beauty and the Beast*—including the tall ladder that rolled back and forth so you could climb up to reach the highest of the leather-bound collections that his father had been collecting for years. That house took my breath away. I felt as if I had just walked into a castle, and my heart rate picked up as everything inside of me started screaming to get out. I didn't belong there, and I knew it—but my God I wanted to belong there! What a dream!

Just after that, we were engaged . . .

Whoa . . . what? Engaged? So it would be all mine? Really?

My editor is now yelling at me to explain myself, and I find it really funny that I've completely glossed over this, because yes, we did get engaged, really fast, and it happened in October, 2005. We met, we dated, we had sex, we got engaged, and we moved in together all in the span of three months. Two months later we would be married, but I'll get to that at a later point.

There were so many factors from both ends encouraging us to get married quickly. Our passion for each other felt electric from the very beginning, and I was in desperate need for someone to show me love and affection. Almost immediately after we started dating, we started shopping for rings at the mall. We told his parents our plans, and his mom encouraged us to just go for it! That was surprising even to me, but her logic was that of a hippy living freely in the moment. My reasons were that I didn't know how much longer my mother would be alive and I wanted her there to see that my life was finally working out. That, and I really needed to get the fuck away from her. Two birds, one really shiny stone on my ring finger. Shawn was the answer to all of my problems. I recognize that that sounds malicious, and it might have been if I did it for all of the wrong reasons—but nothing about it felt that way. Everything felt right, even the way in which he proposed. He bought the ring we had picked out together, came to my home without my knowledge, handed both Mom and Grandma Jane their own bouquets of fresh cut flowers, and asked their permission to marry me. He won over their hearts, and they were elated. On a beautiful October evening he took me on a drive—to where? I bet you can guess. He drove us to that cliff I so often found myself looking over. He got down on one knee as the sun set behind the mountains and asked me to be his wife. Of course, I said yes. It was the greatest thing to happen to me in all my life. I had found a man who truly loved me and wanted to save me from the life I was living, and share his life with me. How could I want anything else? I never second guessed it, not even for a moment. I needed it. I didn't realize how desperate I was, and I probably was confusing my desperation with excitement, but that excitement masked all other emotions that I would not recognize until many years later.

RAISED BY NARCOTICS—Why Your Decisions Don't Matter

After we were engaged, Shawn once again took me to his parents' overly large, and incredibly intimidating, home for my future mother-in-law's annual Halloween party. I was told it was NOTHING compared to other parties Jo had thrown, but even so, the sheer amount of people, decorations, and the buffet she had put together—wow. Now, I love Halloween, and because I was so intimidated by everything going on around me, I desperately wanted to fit in. So, I dressed up, both for the fun of it and to impress his family, showing I had put some real thought into it. I wanted to have a good time and belong to this rich family that was showing me a good time and accepting me as their own so soon after meeting their son. What I didn't know was that Shawn hated these parties and was only doing it because his friends would be there, and he had been told to bring me so everyone could get to know me. I dressed as a black fairy, had my nails done, and put on my cheap costume from Wal-Mart that turned out to be a little sluttier than I had intended. Shawn, on the other hand, didn't dress up at all. That was the first time in our short relationship that I had wanted to strangle him, but I used it to get on his family's good side and ribbed him for it the entire night, laughing with his friends and family, all of whom had dressed up. Honestly, I love this memory, and to this day I give him a hard time for it. He dresses up for every Halloween now (wink emoji).

By November, his parents had helped us pick out an apartment down the street from the apartment Shawn shared with some other students going to the same university. We moved in together. My mother cried while I packed, stopping to hug me way too often and sobbing, "I didn't think you would actually leave me!" (Something we learned to laugh about later.) We all knew why I was moving so fast. I found an out—the same out Mandy had found a few months before—and I was taking it.

We were married on January 4th, 2006. We felt truly made for each other. Our chemistry together was unlike anything I had ever experienced before. It was insane to me. I didn't know such a thing existed in this life. I was happier than I could remember being in the last decade of my life. Life was working, but not because I was working for it. I had gotten lucky.

My life after that became a Cinderella story. His parents sent us to Maui for our honeymoon, and I fell madly and deeply in love with the ocean that I was meeting for the first time. We came back to a home full of groceries—his mom's gift to us—and we picked out a puppy that we named after the stars, Orion. Now, I had a new family. I was free. Finally, and truly, free to start a life that I could be proud of and forget everything that had happened before.

Was it too good to be true? Well, I was nineteen then, and I'm thirty-two now, and we're still married—but I will tell you that we have been through hell together. This is far from the end of this story, but I'll have to fast forward through some of it to get to the points I'm trying to make.

Almost immediately after our wedding, my family accused me of marrying Shawn for his money. Would you blame me if I had? Truth be told, I didn't. He was the first

RAISED BY NARCOTICS—Why Your Decisions Don't Matter

person in my life to care about me in a way no one else did. And, yes, he had a car, and an apartment, and a family who actually offered support—but I'll leave it up to you to decide what my motives were, because truly, I don't even know what they were. I was desperate for an escape, and for a family that would actually love me—so maybe there was some truth to my Uncle Karl's words as he whispered to Mom at my own wedding reception just how wealthy my new in-laws were. I guess he had done his research on the wealthy family that far surpassed his own wealth. I had never liked my Uncle Karl, and that he had done this on my wedding day was something I felt was a huge betrayal. Not that it came as much of a surprise. I have several memories of him barging into Grandma Jane's home and yelling at both me and my mother that we were leaches on his mother, and that she needed to put her foot down and kick us out. This man thought very highly of himself, and quite literally thought that my mother and I were scum—and yet, here I was being embraced by a far wealthier family. You can bet your ass I was happy to hear that it was stinging him just a little bit. We shouldn't have laughed, but Mom and I spent some time after I came home from my honeymoon gossiping over everything he had told her about my new in-laws the day of my wedding. But for as much as we bonded over Karl's jealousy, his words got into her head, and not too long afterward I started hearing how selfish I was for not sharing the wealth that I had married into.

Now I was just the girl who had gotten lucky. Any pride I might have felt in attempting to sort out my own life was blown right out the window. I was quickly becoming a selfish and spoiled bitch to the family I had both tried so very hard to escape and done everything I could to prove myself to.

I started my marriage with an incredible amount of baggage that got worse in ways I could never have predicted. No matter what I did . . . I just didn't do any of it right. Somehow, I had managed to become a worse person in my family's eyes. I shouldn't have cared what anyone thought of me. The point was to get the hell out, and I had, so why did it all bother me so damn much? I couldn't seem to answer that question.

CHAPTER 15

The Four-Year Curse

I'm superstitious. It was hard not to be in my family. When I got married, I immediately took my husband's last name—less out of tradition and more out of superstition. I did not grow up religious. I went to church a few times with Grandma Jane, but it wasn't for me. I am now an atheist, but this isn't about my religious views. It's about superstitions, curses, and things we can't see. Let me explain.

When I was a kid, Mom was convinced that she was clairvoyant. She thought she could see and communicate with dead people and predict the future. Because of this, I was terrified of my own home. She made me terrified of what lurked in the dark. She was convinced that our home was haunted, with a portal right outside my bedroom door (of course).

Her "clairvoyance" made me very scared of the world. I trusted my mother who said dead people were everywhere—and wanted to hurt us—and everyone was trying to convert me to believe in a man in the clouds, which made what she said seem more real, less crazy. I prayed, a lot, for those ghosts to stop haunting me, and asked God continually to give me a break in life. I was about fifteen when I stopped praying. I think you can understand why.

My entire family was superstitious, and I still am to this day. Mom was always commenting on what was, or was not, good luck. This included everything from black cats crossing your path, stepping under ladders, sneezing three times, or making wishes on eyelashes that have fallen onto your cheeks. Everything was a sign. A good omen, a bad omen—and there were a lot of bad omens. It didn't help that the career path I wanted involved a centuries-old civilization that revolved around curses and superstitions. In my downtime, I spent hours upon hours on the Travel Channel, Discovery Channel, and the History Channel watching all the documentaries that showcased ancient Egypt. Since the age of nine, I have been fascinated by mummies and everything else that went along with archaeology. I felt destined to become an archaeologist; it was my ultimate dream in life. I was completely fascinated by all aspects of it, most especially the long-dead human remains and stories upon stories of how these ancient cultures lived. While in high school, I had done some research to see what it would take to become one. My options seemed incredibly limited, and there was always the annoying factor of tuition expenses. Simply put, I could never have afforded it, no matter what my dream had been. Suffice it to say, however, it played a huge role in my superstitions—in addition to Mom's

RAISED BY NARCOTICS—The Four-Year Curse

mental illness. She was never formally diagnosed, but I would put good money that there was some misfiring in the network of her brain.

Shawn now teases me for being what is probably the only superstitious atheist on the planet (I'm sure I'm not, I should start a Facebook group).

We all believed our last name was cursed. Those who bore the Nielsen name were doomed, and shedding that name was very important to me. Is it really necessary to explain that? I mean, just look at the life we were living together. Uncle Karl, however, shared the same last name and look at his life. He's completely fine. Right? He and his family were the rich relatives who had it all. The curse was silly—or was it?

Mom never gave me a middle name so that I could carry my maiden name in front of my married name if ever I chose to get married. This was a very specific family tradition handed down by one of my great grandmothers. I didn't love that choice of hers, because I didn't have a beautiful last name as it was—not like Grandma Jane whose maiden name was Diamond. Of course, Mom was upset when I made the decision to drop the Nielsen name altogether, but why on earth would I carry around a curse on purpose? Dropping it, though, didn't change anything. My life was very slowly getting better, but it was just the calm before the storm.

Let's talk about the "four-year curse." Shawn and I had been married for two years, welcoming our first baby—a girl named Aryn Teresa—in 2007. We bought our first house that spring, thanks to the recession and Ray and Jo's inability to sell the lots they had been developing. We got lucky, time and time again. My husband has his own superstitions and says he lives a charmed life. Luck. We've joked over the years that it's his constant luck and my cursed history that seem to balance out our lives and make us normal.

During this time, I bounced around from job to job. I was focused on being a mom, figuring myself out, trying new hobbies, etc. I never finished hair school (and I had my stupid justifications for this decision). But then, in June 2008, I got a phone call about a job that I'd applied for. I had been waiting and waiting, almost positive I wouldn't get it. It was a receptionist job, two days a week, almost nothing, but it would allow me to be home with my little girl (who was one year old now) and let Shawn focus on his studies while he worked part-time. It was the balance we needed, and they said yes. I was over-the-moon excited.

Unfortunately, my training schedule demanded that I be there full-time for the first week, so I needed someone to watch Aryn. I called Grandma Jane to see if she could do it. She was still working, but she assured me that for at least one or two of those days she would call off and come to our new home and play with the baby that had become her absolute joy. Giving my grandmother a great-granddaughter was a seriously special gift, although Aryn was certainly not the first great grandchild she had. But watching Grandma play with any baby, mine especially, seemed to give her a new energy and joy in life. Grandma Jane was a

RAISED BY NARCOTICS—The Four-Year Curse

baby-hog, and did not want to share, so I had to be prepared every time I came over with little Aryn that I wouldn't get to hold her while she played countless games of patty cake and peek-a-boo with Great-Grandma Jane Diamond.

Grandma Jane made every excuse she could to spend time with the two of us. That spring we went to the park numerous times so that Grandma Jane could push Aryn on the swings and make faces at her while Aryn giggled. We explored the gorgeous gardens at the very place where I was now about to become a receptionist. Grandma Jane would carry Aryn in one arm, point to all the flowers with the other, name every single one of them, then dip her face into the roses so she could smell their beautiful scent.

On the day that Grandma Jane was scheduled to come babysit Aryn, I got a call from Mom saying that Grandma Jane couldn't come because she had woken up with a terrible headache. I told her to call me back later and let me know how she was doing. I still had to be at work, so I sat at my new desk and called around for a different sitter while Shawn sat at home with Aryn, waiting to go to work. Ray and Jo maybe? No, they were in Hawai'i. Not even five minutes passed before I got another call from Mom saying that Aunt Sylvia was there to drive Grandma Jane to the hospital, just to have her checked out. I started worrying, of course—it wasn't normal for Grandma Jane to be sick. She was never sick. In all the years I had known her, the worst thing she had ever suffered from was depression, and that seemed reasonable. Grandma Jane was a workhorse, and the healthiest person in our family. She was fit and active and worked full-time. She was the only person I knew who took joy in home-grown vegetables, and she occasionally cooked meals just for herself because no one else would eat the healthy things she liked.

Now she was on her way to the hospital for a headache? That wasn't okay. Not even an hour later, I got a third phone call. Grandma Jane had a stroke, and we needed to go the hospital. Mom was completely freaking out. I had to leave my brand-new job, asking Shawn to stay home with baby Aryn for the day so I could be the pillar of strength Mom needed me to be. Again.

When we arrived at the hospital, life stood still for a little while. It was explained to us that while Grandma Jane was having her head scanned for potential problems due to her headache, she had a massive stroke. The blood vessels in her brain burst right there. She was brain-dead already.

So many things happened that I could not process them at all once. After Teresa died in 2004, two other family members had passed away.

In April of 2006, right after Shawn and I were married, Grandpa Bill passed away of natural causes and what was essentially old age. Of course, this wreaked havoc on Mom. She had to watch the man who had been her best friend die, but it hadn't been sudden—it was almost expected. He had begun hallucinating about his dead wife, Grandma Erma, and becoming increasingly delirious. It had only been a matter of time, and, of course, time never disappoints. Two weeks after that, Uncle Karl committed suicide. He had hung himself one Sunday morning in the basement of his

RAISED BY NARCOTICS—The Four-Year Curse

home while his family was at church. I never liked Uncle Karl, and in my opinion, the world was well rid of a giant douche bag who had hurt my mother years before I was born and continued harassing my family because of our circumstances. He never seemed like the type of man to help, only another bully in our lives. I resented him immensely, most especially for what he had done to our family right before he cowardly fled from his mistakes.

Growing up, there were always two sides of our family: my family, and Karl's family. Two very different worlds that I did not like to mesh together. Once Grandpa Bill passed away, there seemed to be a direct tear right down the middle of our two families. Uncle Karl did a great job taking over as executor and making sure that my mother did not see a dime of what Grandpa Bill had left behind, nor anyone else for that matter. He took everything, put it all in his wife's name, and then killed himself. It wasn't enough for our family to grieve the loss of a man who had played such a large role in our lives—mine included, him being the only father figure I had really ever known—but Karl took everything, quite literally, to his grave. There was nothing my family could do to get any of it back, and I fumed for weeks over it. Years, really. I mean, I'm still pretty upset about it, but I was nineteen when it happened and pretty naïve about the situation. It's a little difficult for a newly-married teenage girl to wrap her head around her mother's ranting and try to find justice over a problem she doesn't properly understand. But all the problems landed on me when it came to my mother, of course, and I felt like a guard dog trying to protect her. And dammit, I tried. I tried, but I failed after Karl's son decided to rip me a new one because I had made a call to my Aunt April the day after Karl's funeral.

God dammit Karl, it was just too convenient for you to kill yourself so my family would never have what they needed, wasn't it?!

I later found out that he was bipolar, just like Teresa. Well, that fucking explains everything, but it still does nothing to get back what was taken from my family when they needed it most.

Despite this drama in our family, those two deaths didn't count for the four-year curse plaguing my side of the family. What was happening within the walls of my home was something very different. Whatever Karl went through in life, I'll never know. I should probably have more sympathy for what he and his family went through, and if we had been a more supportive network of people, maybe we could have helped him through his trials in life. And who knows, maybe he and his family could have been there for us. Instead we let our differences divide us, and we all chose sides. Each of us thought that we were in the right, but I see now that we were all very much in the wrong. No one wins this way, and it's clear now that none of us did. Who's to blame for any of it? Do we just chalk this one up to the mental illness that was seemingly all over that generation of our family?

That mess played a huge part in how we would handle Grandma Jane's death. *Her death.* She was lying in a

RAISED BY NARCOTICS—The Four-Year Curse

hospital bed, dying. Mom was freaking out and kept saying, "What's going to happen to me now?" You see, at this point she was bedridden with lupus, right? Much too sick for real work, but also much too fly-off-the-handle to bring into my home to be around my one-year-old daughter—to say nothing of all her various bottles of prescription drugs. There was no way in hell I was letting my daughter get even so much as a glimpse into the life I had grown up in.

I didn't have time to grieve the death of the most important woman in my life because I had to think through what would happen to the other woman sitting in a chair next to Grandma Jane, a cane next to her. My insides were in shock. Just that morning Grandma Jane was supposed to be coming to my house to babysit my daughter, and now she was lying in a bed, with that same rattle in her throat as Teresa four years earlier. I would never get to hear her speak or see her smile and laugh ever again. I could not process what was happening.

As family started arriving—Aunt Sylvia with Mandy and her husband; Cody and his wife—we all started arguing about whether or not to let anyone else know this was happening and let them come see her before she finally passed away. Cody and I said, "Absolutely not." It was ultimately Mandy's husband that shared his words of wisdom. He said that despite how Karl's family had acted, Grandma Jane had been the thread connecting us, and she would have wanted to give them the chance to come and show their respect. And so, the phone calls began, and slowly they trickled in—although Karl's widowed wife stayed away.

In Grandma Jane's death, we tried to put our differences behind us. We all stayed as late as we could, Mandy and I making a point to stay with Grandma Jane until everyone on the other side of the family had left the hospital for the night. I think we stayed until around two in the morning. It got to a certain point where we just couldn't keep our eyes open. I was in the midst of a constant anxiety attack, one I feel even now as I write out (and relive) the moment. My muscles shake as if I've been left out in the snow for too long, and I can't quite catch my breath.

Mom too was having a panic attack that night, and she needed to get some sleep. Cody had volunteered to stay the night, along with Aunt Sylvia, to see it through. We made a promise to come back first thing in the morning if nothing changed, but just after 5 a.m., Grandma Jane took her last breath. Later Cody would tell me that she had one tear fall from her face as she passed on. I could sense that he had wanted to hold onto that tear and never let it go. It symbolized so much in the life we had all led together, and in that moment, we both lost the real mother who had raised us and given us what we had needed in life when Diane, our birth mother, was continually falling apart. The big question that came next was: what do we do with Mom now?

We were fortunate in that Grandma Jane recognized that her time was coming to an end, and we all shared our stories of how she was subtly letting us know. She was organizing family photos and calling us all over to take what

RAISED BY NARCOTICS—The Four-Year Curse

she had to give us. I received boxes of photos as well as her good china. The same china set that belonged to her mother, my Great-Grandma Diamond. She would make jokes about how she didn't have much time left, and I guess when you're in your early seventies, your mortality becomes more real. Her sister had died at the age of seventy-two, and now Grandma Jane would as well. Maybe she had predicted this? Maybe it was just a precautionary fear, but with that fear came preparedness, and she didn't want our family falling apart under the burden of funeral costs. After losing Teresa, she had bought a plot right next to her and made payments for her funeral. Mom had done the same thing, always going on about how she was going to die any day now. I believe in these moments she wished it had been her and not Grandma Jane, because without Grandma Jane, Mom couldn't survive—unless one of her children took her in, and neither of us would.

The four-year curse was not over yet, but at this time I didn't yet recognize its effect.

CHAPTER 16

The Next Four Years

When Grandma Jane passed away, I was about to turn twenty-two. A sad fact is that she passed away on Mandy's twenty-second birthday, a month before my own. It's not something we talk about. Cody actively tried to make it seem like she passed in the night before Mandy's birthday, but we were there well past midnight, and even though we put some sleep between us and what happened, it couldn't change what day it was. I wanted to put a positive light on it for the sake of my best friend. If I were to believe in soul mates, I would believe that she is mine. Mandy and I were raised as if we were twins, given how close our mothers were and how close our birthdays are. She's not just a cousin. She's not just a best friend. She's my world. She's my person. I cannot imagine a life without her in it. Grandma Jane raised me like a mother and passed away on Mandy's birthday. Having these two women, the two most important women in my world, share a day has to mean something. Mandy is by far the closest person I can think of

RAISED BY NARCOTICS—The Next Four Years

who resembles Grandma Jane. Quiet, yet stubborn. She'll do absolutely anything for her family, no questions asked. In some ways, they are one in the same. The same weird sense of humor that no one else ever gets to see, until you peel away those layers and literally spend years getting to know them. To honor them both on the same day is fantastic. To know Mandy is to know Grandma Jane.

My point is that we were very young. My little Aryn had only just turned one a few months before. I was still a brand-new mother—and let's be real, a brand-new wife. Now I faced the hardest task in my life, trying to be anything like Grandma Jane and take care of the most difficult person I had ever known—my mother.

Mom and I fought constantly. So badly that Cody and I would fight as well. Everyone was stressed out and no one could agree on anything. We had our good moments, but they were few and far between. It felt like months or years between good moments. I could not understand Mom and what she was going through. I tried. I wanted to be a loving and supportive daughter, but everything I did was wrong, everything I said was wrong. What I think this boiled down to was the fact that I hadn't taken her into my home after Grandma Jane passed away. I had room for her, plenty of room. I had an extra bedroom that we weren't using at all, with her name written all over it, but I just couldn't imagine bringing her there and living with her again. It terrified me so much, so I decided to have a long and endless silence hanging between us rather than try and take care of her. In my mind, she was a grown-ass adult who refused to take care of herself. I saw that she had made her choices and she was living in them, and I judged her for it. Harshly. That didn't take away my absolute love for this woman, or the fact that I needed her approval like I needed air in my lungs.

I was suffocating with and without her.

This doesn't give her enough credit as a human being. She was absolutely delightful at times, and she understood me in a way that no one else did. She understood my sense of humor, she understood my cynicism, and she let me ramble about damn near anything—but man those rambles were dangerous, and she would probably hunt me down for writing this book while simultaneously being so proud she can't breathe. She was a constant ebb of happy and angry. This is why I had such a hard time with everything she was becoming.

Mom had lupus. Mom had thyroid problems. Mom had depression. Mom had post-traumatic stress disorder. Mom had insomnia. Mom had anxiety and restless leg syndrome. Mom took pills for each one of those things, and on top of that Mom had lost four out of six of her immediate family members (Teresa, Grandma Jane, Grandpa Bill, Uncle Karl), and I can bet anything she didn't have the first clue how to emotionally deal with any of it.

How do I explain my mother? She was what anyone ever can be in this life—just struggling to get through it. She loved, unconditionally. Her love was immense and powerful—jolting, really. When she loved you and you could feel it, the world shattered. This world could not contain the type of love she could give. Even she couldn't handle the

RAISED BY NARCOTICS—The Next Four Years

love she felt, and way too often she cried because of it. What a strange thing that is to feel in such a person. To know that they love you with everything they are, but to see them hating just as much. I didn't understand that hate.

As the saying goes: "Hurting people hurt people." Mom was a bully. A bully who just needed love. I saw that, and I tried to give her what I thought she needed, but it was just never enough. Not in the way she needed it. Maybe if I had been able to be a different person for her. A more patient person. A less judgmental person.

The thing here is this: she was my mother—not the other way around. Yet, she needed me to be her mother, and when I tried, she hated me for it. She wanted her independence so badly, but she needed someone to make it easy for her to be what she wanted. I misunderstood so much of what she was going through. Maybe that's why I can't fully describe who she was, because even still, she is an enigma to me.

God, I loved that woman.

So, I didn't let Mom move in with me after Grandma Jane was gone. Had we been a normal family, I certainly would have, but I was afraid of her. I had spent the most important part of my adolescence trying to get away from her, and I couldn't imagine bringing her into my home. I was faced with this hideous decision multiple times in the coming four years.

First, Mom began confiding in a neighborhood friend who had pulled some strings with the LDS Church and found her a place to live just down the street in a home that sat vacant as the owner, another member of the church, was debating what to do with it. At this point, Mom's monthly income consisted of her social security income, Medicaid, and workmen's compensations checks (which she received from the PTSD diagnosis after being sexually harassed on the job). She was considered a disabled person, and no longer had a car to drive. I don't recall when she lost her license, but it's a good thing she did. She relied on people to get around—me, Aunt Sylvia, Cody, sometimes Mandy—but I'm jumping a little ahead of myself. Eventually a for-sale sign was placed in the front yard of the home we had all grown up in. The home that Grandpa Bill had built for his young family so long ago, where hopes and dreams went to die. So much trauma, abuse, and neglect had happened inside those walls.

Because Grandma Jane had been forced to take out a second mortgage after Teresa's accident, the bank was foreclosing on our family home. No one had the money to take care of it, and none of us could afford to keep it for Mom. I'm sure there were some people in our family who had debated if they could take it, but our lives were progressing elsewhere. It didn't make sense to hold onto it. Once Grandma Jane was gone, I could hardly get myself to step foot inside the door. Not the front door, nor the backdoor through the kitchen where anyone who was family entered without knocking. I could no longer step across that threshold. It didn't feel right, and there was nothing inside that I wanted. I know that Cody loaded up what furniture he could and stored it in the basement of his home, but not

RAISED BY NARCOTICS—The Next Four Years

many of us, aside from Mom and her own personal belongings, took anything else. Many things were left behind, and where those things go in situations like this, I have no idea. And I don't really care to know, because I don't want to think about what anyone thought of the possessions we left behind. Teresa's hospital bed that sat empty all of those years later. All of her things. We never went through any of it. All of it, just gone.

And so, we packed up Mom to move down the street. Cody packed while I organized and arranged Mom's new home. For the first time in a long time, I think Mom felt wonderfully independent. She was truly alone now. Her two children were grown and raising their own families, and she was no longer under the thumb of her now-dead mother. The bickering over space and who got to have what set up in the home was now entirely up to Mom, because it was hers alone. She was now the one in control.

But it wouldn't stay that way. Eventually the owner of the home Mom was staying in would decide to demolish it and build something bigger. Mom had to move again, and again a different family within the ward (the neighborhood church community, for those non-Mormons reading this!) took pity on Mom and let her rent out the basement of their home. It was only two houses down from the one being demolished, so moving this time was a little easier, but emotionally it was getting harder to handle. Again, Cody and I were faced with the decision to take in our mother, and I think we each secretly wished the other one would just take her off our hands. Solutions were in place, though, so neither of us did that, but the guilt Mom laid down as we moved her again was set in place, and the manipulation through her emotional stress continued.

On to Mom's third home: her apartment in Provo, Utah. How we got there was painful, and I was nearly convinced that this time she would have to move in with us. How she got that apartment I don't know. Lenient landlord? People demand too much in this world. I had helped her look at a tiny studio apartment that she absolutely could afford, but she just didn't qualify. Once again, I don't know how people do this. I had flashbacks of my own struggles trying to find a small place to call my own once I was an adult and trying to flee the confines of my broken household. Mom was alone and couldn't do these things anymore, and despite being a grown adult woman, she couldn't remember how to take care of herself. She could absolutely sense that I didn't want her in my home, and it put even more strain on our already rocky relationship. Sometimes she grinned and bore it, and other times she screamed it at me that I wasn't truly family. She said that I was still horrible and cruel. One I just had to laugh at was when she called me "hoity toity." She believed that I thought I was too good for her. To a certain degree, she was right. They say—and by "they," I'm probably referring to internet memes—if it's toxic, get away from it. But did you escape your own mother? I simply couldn't be around her, and not because I was better than she was—but because there was something truly toxic about her.

RAISED BY NARCOTICS—The Next Four Years

As I reflect on these moments, I recall her becoming more withdrawn, and I wonder if it was the isolation that she was now facing. I saw her less and less. We still argued plenty—and I still tried to be the good daughter and rise above our problems enough to be there for things like groceries, doctor appointments, etc.—but I was becoming disconnected from my own family. It was a rare occasion to see Cody and Cara and their two daughters. Family, as I knew it, changed drastically. I started inviting Mandy and her growing family (she eventually had a little girl named Sophia, who is only three years younger than Aryn) to Jo's infamous parties, and to my new family's home. Occasionally Cody would come as well, but family gatherings for us were becoming non-existent.

How did I feel through all of this? I felt lost and heartbroken. I honestly remember the horrible fights we continued to have, and feeling completely helpless as I would drive home, not knowing who to confide in. Would Shawn just be upset with me that it wouldn't stop? Would he resent that Mom and I could never agree on anything, and I was just so sick of being told how wrong and horrible I was? He was always understanding, but it ate at me, and it ate at our marriage. It wore us both down to the point where my baggage came up in our fights together, and I just felt like I was ruining any chance he had at living up the potential that his rich parents had provided for him. Mom was still ruining my life, and now his—and I wanted her to disappear.

It became bad enough that we would ignore each other for months at a time. If I could guess, I would say we spoke to each other something like 30% of the time. Maybe that's overly dramatic, maybe it was larger—but recently I sat down to look through my photos from this time in our lives (now that everything is digital, it's much easier to go through then sitting and digging through albums), but do you know what I found? Only handfuls of images in the entire four years, and you know how much we all rely on our little camera phones in this new age. Maybe that percentage is smaller. It hurts all over. It hurts so much. You don't think that the pain of it can creep into your life after all these years, but there it is. It's not a pain I can describe, so I'll wipe my tears and move on with my story.

CHAPTER 17

Clueless

Everyone was fighting. I was fighting with mom. I was fighting with Cody *about* Mom. I was fighting with Shawn about our life together and which one of us was going to take opportunities in life. Aryn was little and we couldn't afford daycare, and we had decided that it wasn't something we wanted her to know. I had my own personal reasons for wanting her to know a good and supportive family, and Shawn didn't think that it made sense to pay someone else to raise our child, especially not with the kind of money he came from. Essentially one of us had to stay home with her while the other got an education and worked towards a career. To an extent, we switched between the two of us depending on the circumstances.

We had Shawn's parents helping us with various financial aspects, but we weren't the rich people that Mom thought we were. I couldn't just plan vacations and head out to who-knows-where and beach it up—but Shawn's mom Jo could, and she brought us with her. We went on a cruise to Mexico and the Caribbean when I was pregnant with Aryn. She had already sent us to Maui on our honeymoon, and had started taking us to both Disneyland and Disney World, where we most certainly did beach it up on both the California and Florida coastlines. On top of that we had many shopping trips where hundreds, if not thousands, of dollars were spent on baby clothes for my new little girl and entire new wardrobes for myself. Not to mention when Aryn was three, Jo flew us out to San Francisco to meet up with an artist friend of their family, the same one who had painted those lavish paintings of Jo and Ray hanging above their grand piano in their foyer. They had one for each of their six children lining the walls of their castle-like home, and now one for my sweet little princess. They also commissioned Lynn, the painter, to update the portraits for their six children. Each of those paintings cost between $20,000 and $40,000. I don't think I'm supposed to know this, and when I found out, I was already so submerged in the lifestyle that it hardly fazed me, but there's a price tag hanging on the back of a couple of them. What would I have done had I known their value when the paintings were happening? I mean flying to California was well above my luxurious lifestyle expectations, but this would not have been something I could wrap my head around. This is the family I married into. The family that could spend hundreds of thousands of dollars on updated portraits of their grown children just because they thought it was neat to have. Can you imagine that kind of money?

RAISED BY NARCOTICS—Clueless

What's my point? That shit is hard to get used to, and I had the trouble of being both a part of it and being seriously removed from it. What can I even liken this to? I was a member of their family, but it was not my family and it was not my money—it was my husband's family and his parent's money, but not his money. None of it belonged to us directly. I got to enjoy it if it was offered, but I could in no way ask for it. Shawn and I butted heads over this thousands of times. Many of our arguments were about this. He was their oldest son. There's a lot of entitlement that comes with that in a wealthy family, and yet I wanted us to be independent because of how I had grown up. I wanted desperately to have pride in what we were making for our little family, but it was all unnecessary.

Look, up until this point in my life, I had never been prepared for the situation where I would marry a millionaire's son.

Lucky bitch.

I know!

This was Mom's perspective of us. Of me. I was the rich bitch not making lavish donations to my family, but how was I supposed to do that? It wasn't mine in any way, shape, or form. I made the mistake of asking for it once, early in my marriage, and I believe it was deeply traumatic—not only for me (obviously), but also for my new relatives. It became something I would no longer discuss with them. It wasn't my right, and I had to learn my place, which was— and I had to decide this for myself because there were no guidelines or expectations set forth for me to follow—that I was damn lucky to have married into such a wealthy family.

Of course, I wanted the things their money could buy me and my daughter. Who wouldn't want that? I didn't have to worry about anything anymore. After arguing about it fiercely, Shawn and I quickly decided that I would not bring up money or needs in that department. He would do it, but only if he saw fit to. It wasn't really his decision—I flat out refused to discuss money with his parents. It wasn't mine, and I had to live life assuming I was still poor and married to a broke college student with weird financial benefits. I hated feeling beneath him and his rich life, and yet above my own family. The whole thing was strange.

I was feeling torn between my two worlds, like an outsider to both. Where did I belong? What was the right thing to do, or accept, or to ask for? How could I help my mother if I couldn't ask for money? How did I fit into this big wealthy family? Should I act like it wasn't a big deal, or act humble enough that they didn't always assume that's what I wanted? I felt desperate for my new family to accept me as their own, to truly be a new daughter in their family. Yet, I also felt desperate to help my own mother rise above her impossible circumstances. I was terrified that she would see me as cruel, and I couldn't stand being the cruel daughter. What choices did I make for myself? For my little family? For my mother? There were so many perspectives to this situation—so in the end, who's point did I concede to? There was no right. There was only wrong.

RAISED BY NARCOTICS—Clueless

In the end, I tried to isolate myself from these people and their differing perspectives. I didn't know how to show how massively important they were to me, other than to remove myself. I no longer wanted to bother them with my inability to be the person they expected me to be. I tried acting as if I were a single mother with no family.

What would that person do in my situation?

She would go back to school, get some form of education, and raise her daughter. So, I did. I went back to hair school, after realizing that I couldn't justify to myself the reasons why I had quit twice before.

I was so confused about where I fit into the bizarre puzzle that was my life, so I tried to distance myself and build my own from pieces I picked up here and there.

Despite how removed I wanted to be, it wasn't actually possible. The fights continued, both with Mom and with Shawn. That's the hard part. Mom wasn't trying at all to see my perspective, and everything I said she used against me. I once said, "Mom, I can't give you that money because the only money I have is saved up for Aryn and the things she needs." And she blew it all out of proportion.

"I would never take money from my granddaughter! How dare you accuse me of that!" But I hadn't been accusing her of it. She twisted my words and my meanings, and I always felt like I had failed her or said something so incredibly offensive. How could I live with myself? I knew I shouldn't have her in my life, but how could I divorce my sick and dying mother? How cruel does a person need to be to abandon the only family they have—especially when they need them the most?

This is what I was up against. Then I did something truly stupid, and accidentally found my father.

CHAPTER 18

Ben

This is a dot in my past. A dot that reappears just within the periphery of my vision every so often.

I didn't mean to find my father. I had tried to, years before, during a computer class in high school. I searched his name on the internet, and I found some information on him, but it required a credit card and there was no way I could spend whatever amount they were asking. I wasn't even sure if I truly wanted him in my life. (What would have changed if I could have Facebook stalked him back then? I was about three years too early. Social media as we know it today—whether you love it or hate it—didn't exist back then.) There was no finding my father unless I was serious, and I wasn't. I didn't have the self-esteem to be serious, and I kept hoping he was just dead. What I knew about him was that he had Type-1 diabetes. It was a disease that I probably wouldn't get, but it might affect my children. Mom had always hoped it had killed him or made him blind. I assumed he was a dirtbag, dead or living on the streets. I didn't wish him well, because he had abandoned me before he had ever even known me. He had never even looked at my face. Had he, he might have stayed. Was I cute enough for him to stay? Could I have been a daddy's girl? The way my little girl was now to her father? I had my unanswered questions, but I knew there were ways to discover the truth of something without making contact with the enemy.

My father's mother was from Mexico. So, I have a bit of Mexican blood running through my veins, and stories dating back to the ancient Aztecs via my mother. I've always been the darkest member of my family, and I've enjoyed the uniqueness that it has given me. I couldn't tell you which came first, my obsession with ancient cultures and wanting to become an archaeologist one day, or my obsession with my Aztec roots. I believe the two are strongly intertwined. One leading directly into the other, and because of this fascination I decided to learn Spanish in high school. When Shawn and I took the cruise with his family through Mexico, I wondered how many of my family members resided there. Had I run into any of them? Was I related to the people and culture surrounding me?

I've carried that fascination with me into my adult years, and when I became a mother, I simply wanted more information about those particular roots for the purpose of passing them onto my children and future generations to come.

I knew that it was possible to find out more, and if you know even one Mormon family, then you know at least one pro at family history research. It just so happened that I knew several, so I started by asking my good friend Meghan and her husband Cory for help. I was in luck! They could help me look back in time to see where that half of my family came from, but it all got side tracked when Cory (damn you Cory!) found my father's name on LinkedIn. You know that one, the social media platform for the professional resume builder. He also thought that he might have found him on Facebook, but the profile photo was of a man standing so far away it was hard to make out what he even looked like. Of course, the privacy settings were such that there were no other photos.

In December of 2010, I was just about to graduate from beauty school. I had finally accomplished this obstacle in my life, and here I was realizing that I could use social media to not only find, but maybe even communicate with, my long-lost father who had never so much as bothered to try to find me.

As if I didn't have enough emotional problems to deal with, now I sat in front of my computer, a link to my dad's LinkedIn profile staring right back at me.

Is this book a movie yet?

Was I really sitting here debating whether to reach out to my own dad? After twenty-four years of my life had already gone by? He was this age when I was born. Jesus, he would be nearly fifty at this point. How could that bastard leave me for twenty-four years?! And yet... I knew I desperately needed answers to all of the questions burning a hole in my heart.

I became hopeful, but also terrified. The anxiety came back—or really, it just doubled. It's not as if it had ever left me. I wanted to reach out, but I was terrified. I needed him to *want* to know me, to want to be in my life, to love me. He wasn't a dead beat. He was a normal man with a normal career. He was an IT professional. Maybe he had chosen his career over having a family. Could I begrudge him for that? Family was a difficult thing to live with, and I knew already that I wasn't his first child. His first child—born to a woman who had suffered great mental illness and had run off when things got tough—was born with mental illness as well. Ben (my dad) had tried to be a single father to this growing boy that he couldn't take care of. It was too much to bear alone, and he wasn't strong enough emotionally or financially to handle what his son needed. He gave him up to the state, where he was adopted out to a good Mormon family from Salt Lake City. I had always known about my older brother, Mom called him BJ, but it had never occurred to me to try to find him. Growing up, Mom had told me stories about him because she had known him as a small baby; she had even tried to help Ben care for him before Ben ultimately gave him up for adoption. It was not a decision she had any control over, and I believe this was before they were romantically involved. Perhaps it had been a catalyst for their involvement? I can't say.

Had Ben loved my mother? Had he wanted to have me? Had he been scared that I, too, would be a sick baby? Why had he fled this time around?

RAISED BY NARCOTICS—Ben

Mom told me that he left for the love of another woman. Apparently, this other woman had told him that he could not see me or she would leave him. Had that been true? Or an excuse he had given to my mother out of fear? When I was young, Mom would occasionally get letters in the mail with my father's name on it. I don't know what they said or what they represented. He never paid child support, and from what I knew, no one was out to look for him. All I could do was trust my mother to know what was best and let me know if he ever really wanted a part in my life. Would she have let him if he had tried? *Did* he try?

I wanted answers to all these questions, so here's what I wrote:

Dear Ben,

You may not know me, but you knew my mother, Diane Nielsen. I'm her daughter Alyse, and I believe you're my father. I would love to hear from you if you're interested in connecting.

Alyse Neibaur

I've lost the original message, but it was very short and simple, because I was so scared of how he would respond—or if he would even respond at all. I tried to keep it somewhat professional and lacking in any emotion. Sending it via LinkedIn almost felt like sending a resume.

I noticed your help wanted sign for the position of "daughter." I'm known to be cruel and heartless, but if you give me a chance . . .

That was just before New Year's Eve 2010, and I became completely obsessed with checking my email for a response. On New Year's Day, I actually had to work, but before I was able to head out the door, I finally got it. It came as I walked down our hallway to grab my shoes. He replied something like:

Alyse,

I've always known about you, and so does my family. I'm so happy that you reached out. I would love to talk more and stay connected.

Ben Anderson

So, he had a family.

Here's what came next. He had listed his email address on his profile, and once we were connected on LinkedIn, I used that to communicate with him.

Stay with me here, this will be fun. Maybe a little irrelevant to the overall message of the book I'm writing, but his presence in my life changed my life. For good or for ill, it is what it is.

CHAPTER 19

Letters From Dad

Ben,

There really are no words that can describe just how happy I am to hear back from you. I feel speechless. When I saw your reply this morning . . . I was stunned. I started bawling, a reaction I didn't expect myself to have.

I'm sorry if I have overwhelmed you at all, although I can't expect you not to feel overwhelmed. I myself feel incredibly overwhelmed but also incredibly happy.

Thank you so much for giving me your phone #. I do want to talk to you. My husband and I are going out of town tomorrow and I won't be back until Wednesday night. I think, because of how fast this all happened and how overwhelmed I am, I am going to wait to give you a call until I get back.

I have so much I want to talk to you about. So many things I want to ask you.

Before any of that though, I want to make sure you're okay with this. I've never met you, and I don't know how this all makes you feel. I don't want to over step any *boundaries in my excitement to get to know you. Please let me know.*

Please feel free to email me anytime at all because I would love to hear more from you, and when I get back I will give you a call.

Thank you so much for giving me this opportunity.

Alyse Neibaur

Yeah, that's the email I sent to him the same day he responded. Can you tell I was freaking out? Here's what he said:

Alyse,

It is awesome that you are happy. Sorry you started bawling. My wife tells me that is a girl thing. It is no problem that you wait to give me a call. I am happy that you contacted me. I will be happy to answer all your questions as you deserve that and much more. This is a very cool start to a New Year so let me say for the first time to you and your family . . . Happy New Year!!!

Do not worry about overstepping any boundaries with me. I just want you to have answers to your questions and hopefully we can get to know each other. It is great to hear from you. I feel a bit speechless myself.

Feel free to email me as well and I look forward to communicating with you.

Ben

From there, Shawn and I went on a road trip to celebrate our fifth wedding anniversary in Las Vegas, NV. I couldn't stop thinking about it and all the what ifs. This

RAISED BY NARCOTICS—Letters From Dad

man had a wife, and from the sounds of it a family. Did I have more siblings? What if I had lived with him instead of Mom? What if I had found him in my teen years when everything was falling apart? Would he have taken me in to live with him? Could I have known a different family? All things I rambled at Shawn on our six-hour road trip through the desert.

Ben,

Happy New Year to you too!
Your wife is right, it is very much a girl thing.
I don't know where to start.
You're obviously married . . . the first question that comes to mind is do you have any other children? Do they know about me? Did your wife know about me? How old are they? Assuming you do have other children. Tell me everything! You look so good in the photo I was able to see of you, and you look happy.
I want to know about your life, about you, your personality, your hopes, your family, everything.
Let me tell you a little about me.
I am married, have been for five years on Tuesday the 4th of Jan. Which is why we are going out of town, to celebrate! His name is Shawn, and he is so sweet and amazing.
We have a little girl who will be four in March. Her name is Aryn Teresa, and she did look just like me but somehow, she now has blonde hair and blue eyes like her

daddy. You would love her. Her personality just kills me, and she acts more like an adult than a 3-year-old.

My mom and I still talk. We have a weird relationship but for the most part it's a good one. I will tell you more about that later.

I currently work as a receptionist, as I'm sure you saw. I am also a Cosmetologist. I just finished school for it on Dec 9, 2010. It took me a while, but I'm happier doing that than desk work and hoping my license will arrive soon so I can get a job in a salon.

I love art, music (surprisingly rock and metal are my favorite, soft music makes me cry, I'm too much of a girl I guess), theater, movies, nature, reading, and recently cooking, although I'm not that great at it yet I do plan on improving.

I'm not religious, never found it appealing although I am curious about your own thoughts on that.

I can say I am so much different now than when I was living at home. I've made plenty of my own mistakes, but I corrected them and made a happy life for myself. And I am happy! Very very happy, and happier today than I have ever been thanks to this.

I'm not normally this chatty but I feel like my mind is exploding. I'm sure you have your own questions?! Your own curiosity.

Ask me anything, and tell me everything :)

Alyse

Wow, look at all of that. It's so weird reading my own messages, and you can see that I'm struggling but I'm covering it up because I don't know what this is yet. In retrospect, I should have gone a lot slower, but I had years and years to make up. You can see it as well as I can now: I

RAISED BY NARCOTICS—Letters From Dad

desperately needed him to have interest in me as a daughter and human being.

Alyse,

First of all, CONGRATULATIONS on being married to an awesome guy and having a wonderful daughter. I hope someday I am fortunate enough to meet you all.

Yes, I am married. We have been together for the better part of 25 years. During that time, we got divorced (in 2000) and remarried just a couple of years ago. I have two step-children who are from my wife's previous marriage. We also have a soon to be 21-year-old son. His name is Trenton. My stepdaughter Katrina is having a birthday today, she is 33. John, my stepson, is 35. John has three kids, Billy 16, Katy 13, Susan 10. Katrina has two daughters, Amy 10 and Anna 7. Our son Trenton got married to Jamie two years ago and they have no kids yet.

In case you don't know, we all live in North Idaho. My dad, Nathan, and his wife, Linda, live near here in the mountains (Hoodoo Mountain) about an hour away.

All of the above-mentioned people are aware of you and always have been. I'll bet they would all love to meet you someday.

We are just about to head down the road and I will be back in a bit. I am going to go ahead and hit send just because you are probably dying of curiosity and this is at least part of the story. I can't wait to tell you more and hear more about yourself.

Ben

Would you just look at that huge family? What I've deleted here are all birthdates he included. There's pride there, for his son and his step children. Maybe a rocky marriage, but they are a close family. And my Grandfather Nathan... Everyone knows about me?! And no one, not one person in that family ever reached out? I begin to feel jealous, apprehensive, a little more broken-hearted and lost. How could I not? But the part that hurts the most are the mention of the step-children who knew the father that I never would.

The messaging continues, and I get some answers to my questions:

> The first part of the story is that I obviously dated your mom. We worked at the same place and that is how we met. We only dated a couple of times and then I found out she was pregnant. Unfortunately, I did not love her and originally agreed to pay child support and be a visiting dad. After you were born, I got scared about the whole thing and did not visit. That is my biggest mistake. I met my wife and we had developed a strong relationship and moved to North Idaho together in 1988. I told her about you but I still didn't have the courage to make any contact. I finally tried to contact you around 1995 and the only information I had was my child support contact, so I spoke with them and they told me they could not give me your address or contact info. As an alternative they said I could have them pass along my information, and if you contacted me and it was approved by your mother, then we could communicate. Nothing ever came of that, and rather than pursuing it, I thought I might be intruding at this point. It occurred to me that Diane may have remarried, and

RAISED BY NARCOTICS—Letters From Dad

you had someone who you thought was your father. At that point I decided that I would make myself easy to find and hope that someday you would contact me if that was your wish.

I have always thought of you as my daughter. It is my regret that I wasn't there for you. I know an apology just doesn't cut it but I am very sorry. You certainly deserve more than I have given you and I only hope you are happy as you appear to be. I have neglected my responsibilities and could have done much more to try and contact you. My own fears got in the way. These things I cannot make up for and it leaves me with an empty feeling like I totally dropped the ball for you. At least you can have your questions answered so you don't have to keep on wondering. Anything you would like to know just ask.

So, there's the letter I remember Mom getting. She didn't want me to know about my dad. She didn't want him to be part of our lives. He'd already been gone for nearly ten years of my life at that point. I can understand this. I don't begrudge this. He made a half-assed effort, but what fucking government do we live in where fathers who finally decide to step up to the plate are told "Sorry, no you can't"? Seriously?! *Government, you got some 'splaining to do.*

Here's more:

You never know, you might have found a homeless alcoholic. Actually, I don't like to drink much so I am in little danger of becoming an alcoholic. I am glad you decided to contact me!

So my mother is the Mexican side of things. Her maiden name is Concha Concepcion Saldivar. She was

> born in Brownsville, Texas. I think she has four sisters
> and no brothers. I got to meet my great-grandma when I
> was younger and living in Texas. I can't remember her
> name, but she has quite a story. She was married to a
> general in the Mexican army. General Zamora. It is my
> understanding that he rode with Poncho Villa. They
> were run out of Mexico by jealous relatives who wanted
> their land and money. They killed General Zamora in
> front of his wife and daughter (my mom's mother) and
> ran them out of town, across the border to Brownsville,
> Texas where my mother was born.

So, there it is, a Mexican family history lesson. Pretty neat. Those bastards killed my great-grandfather! I'm not the only one who grew up without a father—so why didn't she set my own father straight?!

Here's a bit more on the history lesson:

> I should tell you that I am not an expert in genealogy
> and what I tell you is probably missing something in
> translation since I am working from old memories. My
> mom, your grandmother, was ½ Mexican and ½ Indian
> (Aztec). Someone did the genealogy and I heard that it
> can be traced to the sister of Montezuma, ruler of the
> Aztecs. I would love to know more but that is as much
> as I know about her side.
>
> Nathan, your grandfather, was born in Kanosh,
> Utah. His family goes back quite a way and some of it
> is well documented. He has five brothers and one sister.
> Mormonism comes from his side of the family. In fact,
> one of our ancestors travelled across the plains with the
> Mormons and Brigham Young and was a hunter and
> provider on the journey. He also met Joseph Smith. His
> name is Lincoln Baxter and there is a book about him

RAISED BY NARCOTICS—Letters From Dad

that my dad has. Nathan's ancestors go back to the origin of this country. They are some of the earliest settlers in the colonies. Your grandpa thinks they came from Ireland or Scotland if I remember correctly.

Curiosity satisfied. I guess. Who knows how accurate any of that is, but hey, it's cool stuff. Stuff I'll save for my children and perhaps one day create a book showcasing our roots with my own genealogy research.

#goals

From there, I go on to chat a little with the father I never knew, and I get to know where some of my personality traits come from. We skype, once, and it's awkward as hell, but shit continues to happen with Mom. I try to explain it to this new man in my life, and I think he does his best to relate and understand, but he just can't—and honestly, he's part of my problem and I begin to realize this. This man should have been my father, and never was. This is on him, not on me. There's nothing I could have done differently in my life to force him to make the right decisions. He didn't want me, and I have to come to terms with that emotional heartache.

I become broken. I've always been a bit broken—how could I not be? But now I'm . . . I don't know. I don't know what I need, who I am, or where I belong, which doesn't seem to be with any of the families that I am connected to. My head hurts, it's spinning, and I can't figure anything out. So, I do what feels right and deactivate my Facebook account. And this, in turn, is the result of that disconnection:

ALYSE NEIBAUR

Alyse,

I see that you have blocked me, I understand and will give you your space. Been nice trying to get to know you. Not sure how I offended you, just by being me I suppose. If it was my wife's email, then I cannot apologize since she is the love of my life and I cannot hold it against her that she wants to get to know you just like I do. We both have a lot of family in Utah and were looking forward to a vacation next year where we could visit with you and others down there. We will still do that without including a visit with you since we seem to make you so uncomfortable.

Just an FYI about your mother . . . she supposedly was on birth control when we were dating. I found out from a good friend of hers (her roommate at the time) that she lied to me about that, so she could trap me and now you know the whole story.

I wish you and your family the best.

Ben

There it is. The truth—or at least his justification for not being the man he should have been despite our circumstances in life. I don't know who to believe, and I don't know if I care. I've never known this man, and all he's done now is prove to me that he would rather place blame on someone else rather than step up and take care of the children he created. He had both admitted to me that he should have been there, and now taken a huge step back and put it all on Mom that the mistake of my life was squarely on her. His true colors.

Fuck you, Ben.

CHAPTER 20

The Things That Break Us

In your lifetime, you'll have moments that define certain paths you end up taking. There are things you'll look back on—and thanks to hindsight, you'll likely learn a great deal from them. You'll decide to either let it make you better, or let it make you fall apart.

I had already experienced quite a handful of things that could have, and maybe should have, broken me. Maybe there was even a time I would have considered myself broken, and had I been a braver person, I would have ended my seemingly meaningless existence. But despite all of this, I am still here. I held onto what love I was given as if I would lose it at any moment, and I tried my very best to rise above the noise in my life. We all have noise. We all have reasons, excuses, justifications to be a certain way. I certainly still do.

It's summer of 2011. Everything is going to happen fast now. When things happen this quickly, it's hard to make good decisions, or right decisions, or any decisions whatsoever.

Where was I in my life at this point? I had quit my awesome receptionist job because I had graduated hair school and was hoping to get a job at a salon. Shawn and I were in the middle of sorting out our own lives, and ultimately, I went from working part-time and going to school part-time, to being a stay-at-home mom to our little girl. Shawn had buckled down and received a bachelor's degree in psychology at the same time I graduated cosmetology. It wasn't his passion, so he didn't pursue anything relating to it beyond getting his degree. The sad truth is he felt obligated to get any degree at all to appease the people around him and prove something. He still had big dreams, so we settled on finding him a job that could provide the benefits we needed as a family, becoming more independent from his family's financial assistance.

Shawn and I were working through our differences, but it was not always easy to see eye-to-eye. From my perspective, he had shot down the idea of me going back to school so many times that I thought he wanted to keep his woman in her place and be the man of the family. I ended up going back to school without his "permission," and I wasn't sure at the end of it if our relationship would survive us both finding ourselves and becoming independent. He always told me that he had so much more potential than I did, so it was about damn time he showed it.

The most important thing to me was that I had finished something I had started. I had proven to the people around me that I could do that.

Hah! In your face! You don't know me!

RAISED BY NARCOTICS—The Things That Break Us

I felt that way toward everyone. Shawn. My mom. His parents. The only person who had pushed me forward into finishing was, you guessed it, Mandy. She stood by me the entire time. This feels significant, I guess. The people around me weren't supporting what I was doing. No one believed in me—that was very clear—and you know what, I guess they were right. They had no reason to believe I could succeed at anything I did. I hadn't done anything to prove it.

Did I believe in me?

So, in the summer of 2011, I wanted my husband to show me that he could take care of our family the way he kept saying he would. Shawn searched for a job and found one that used his natural skills in IT and offered our family some independence and great health benefits. It started making me second-guess my decision to not have any more children (even though I had parted with all of our baby stuff, including the crib). Mom was pissed when I'd given away the bassinet she had gifted to Aryn, even though I gave it to a local charity. She had wanted what she had given to hold deep and significant importance in our lives. I had no more use for it, though, so what was the point? I parted with it without a second thought. The second thought only came after Mom's emotional inability to let go of anything. She and I were worlds different that way. I let go too easily, and she refused to let go at all, but I was the one in the wrong in her eyes.

At this point, Mom was becoming a hoarder, and word had gotten out that she had applied for and maxed out several credit cards, as well as buying things off TV infomercials and going into serious debt. I don't even know how she did this. My experience trying to apply for credit cards was nearly impossible. It was only made possible by Shawn's parents co-signing with us and telling the bank teller, "We have over a million dollars in our accounts here, if that doesn't qualify my son and his wife for a measly $500 credit line, then I guess we take our money elsewhere." And that's where we started, a $500 credit line, and the intimidation of someone else's money forcing people to back down in our favor.

We had to use his mother to threaten a bank teller so we could qualify for a credit card. What the hell was Mom doing? Her apartment was becoming packed with coats, shoes, and toys for her three granddaughters whose visits were becoming less frequent. She bought us all gifts and expected us to be incredibly thankful when she handed them to us, and we had better hold onto that treasure forever or else. Mom was trying to buy our love.

Mom's behavior was becoming worrisome. I mean, more so than ever before. She seemed in her right mind even if she was, well, a bitch. Over the years, I had done a lot of research on lupus, learning that it slowly kills your organs one by one, including your brain. Mom losing her mind was literally going to happen, and it was getting worse all the time. She had been worried that she would lose the function of her legs, now she thought she needed a wheelchair to get around. I refused to hear it and would continue to refuse to hear it until she proved to me that she literally couldn't get out of a chair, or up the stairs. I wasn't going to let her fall apart more than she had. I wanted her to stop justifying her slow decay.

She also refused to eat anything other than cereal, coffee, and ice cream. That was her diet. I attempted to bring her some veggie trays as well as some homemade frozen dinners that she could easily thaw and cook without much effort. I wanted to make life as easy on her as I could, but she refused me most of the time. I can guess that most of what I made for her was thrown in the trash.

And then Mom disappeared. She fucking vanished. Mom didn't trust me at this point. We were fighting a lot again, because I wouldn't be the perfect daughter and cater to her every whim.

She left without warning. She was a grown woman and she could do as she pleased, right? When she left, I was terrified that I might never see her again, and yet I had conflicting thoughts of both hoping she would die somewhere out there and wanting her to come home so desperately that the fear was eating me alive. I had wished she wasn't my mother more than I hadn't, but to actually lose her? That shit is terrifying.

I didn't know what to do. Do I report her as a missing person? Do I clear out her apartment? What do I do? Do I prepare for the worst? The biggest problem I had was that my family knew her better than I did at this point. She had called Aunt Sylvia from Las Vegas. She had called Mandy from Wendover, NV. She had been asking for help with money and a ride home. Eventually she found her way back, but just as quickly she disappeared again. Where the hell was she going?

The second time was even harder. I was convinced I wouldn't see her again. I got a phone call from my brother saying she was gone again, and that I needed to get her pills out of her house so that one of my cousins wouldn't go in there and steal them, which I had heard he had done before. I didn't know what to believe anymore. I didn't know who to trust. Hearing these stories from my mom made me wonder how much she had already lost her mind.

I went to her apartment with the spare key I had secretly made for myself after the first time she had disappeared. Going back into her apartment again was just weird—there's no other description. She was very clearly a hoarder now, having bought tons of coats and shoes that were bursting from her closets. Blankets, toys, and odd things here and there. Eventually, I found her lock box where she kept most of her prescriptions. I didn't have a key to the lock box, but that didn't matter. I knew what was in it, so I took it. Not knowing if she would come back, I also went into her closets and dug around for the boxes of photos and photo albums that Grandma Jane had left to her. I took those, too. Anything that seemed to have any importance, I took.

Eventually, she came back. This was becoming a weird pattern I didn't like. She was gone for about two weeks—it was both the longest two weeks of my life and as if she had never left. This time she came back crazier than before, although now she had a new story of meeting someone, eloping to Las Vegas, finally getting married—she had never done that before—but then he died. That's why he didn't come back. What did he die of? I have no idea. Apparently in his death, though, he had meant to leave Mom money. The money never showed up. He had never been seen by anyone in our family and Mom just went back to life as normal.

I will never know the truth of what happened when she disappeared. I have my guesses, but I'll just never know the answers to the hundreds of questions I have for her.

But she was back. It was nearly fall—her favorite season—and her birthday was approaching. She would turn fifty on October 16th. A man had shown up in her life—a man I knew all too well, the same man who had been breaking her heart for over thirty years. My brother's dad, Steve.

Mom put herself together. She looked nice, happy even. Steve had come to the rescue. He wanted to be with Mom. *What?!* Mom wanted me to bring Aryn over to meet him. I refused to bring her with me. I had no idea what was going on, but Aryn was not going to be around that man.

When I showed up to give Mom her lockbox with her pills, she was all dolled up. She had put on makeup like she used too. She very deliberately covered the scars and sores on her face, arms, and hands with makeup and long sleeves, and she was smiling. He was making her happy. She looked great.

Something was off, though, and I couldn't figure out what. Steve looked happy to see me, but I was very skeptical of him and his sudden reappearance in her life. He always did that, just showed up out of the blue, and no one knew why. I certainly didn't. He expected his charisma to win out, but I wasn't little anymore. It would never win out again.

Just as fast as he had shown up, he was gone again, having to go back to work or something. I don't know what excuse he gave her, but he said he wanted to come back and marry her, properly this time—or so Mom had said to me once he was gone again. She was elated.

At this point, Mom had neglected to pay her rent and was very close to becoming homeless. We had been given stipulations from the Mormon Church on just how much they could help, and she had used up those resources. Mom was losing her mind. I would have been in denial over it, and maybe chalked it up to forgetfulness or stress, but then she told me she had cancer. At a certain point, you cannot be blind to what's happening even if you don't want to see what is right in front of you.

I had come for a visit, with little Aryn, to see what I needed to do to help her get back on her feet when she told me that she had cancer and would be doing chemotherapy soon. Her doctor, the same doctor who had been there to explain to us that Teresa wouldn't be waking up ever again, was the one who diagnosed her. So, when she asked me to take her to her next appointment, I was more than happy to. Happy is absolutely the wrong word, but I needed answers, so accompanying her was the only option.

And thus began the first day of the end of the road for my mother.

CHAPTER 21

A Broken System

I went to Mom's apartment to pick her up for her appointment. I was one of the only people who could take her. She had me, Cody, and occasionally Aunt Sylvia. She had to rotate who she asked, because we all hated going with her. I should have been a better daughter—but I just wasn't. I did my best for her; I truly believe that I did.

When I picked her up for that particular appointment, I had Aryn with me. Once I knocked on Mom's door, and she let me in, I realized how instantly angry she was with me. From the get-go, I was baffled by it. I showed up early—I always showed up early. It's who I am. I am notoriously early to everything I do, probably even annoyingly so. I read in a book once this quote that I loved. It fit me so well.

> *To be early is to be on time, to be on time is to be late, to be late is to be forgotten—Elin Hilderbrand*

My mentality is, what's the harm in being early? Well, when you're dealing with my mother, there's every harm. She was snappy and rude. I couldn't understand it. We were running out of time, and I wanted to help push her along, but she had yet to even get dressed. She was pissed at me for being early.

What?

On the way home, we had both gotten so mad at each other that, for the very first time in my life, I blew up. Completely lost my shit, with my daughter witnessing everything from her vantage in the backseat. All I could hope was that she would block out this memory and be too young to remember that it ever happened. I wanted to die afterwards.

I simply had had enough, and in my having enough, I yelled at her that she was being ridiculous. I told her that I went so far out of my way all the time to help her have what she needed, but she had never been the mother that I needed. I laid my life on the line to be there for her, like she was the child, and then . . .

I said it.

I screamed it.

"I DON'T LOVE YOU! I HATE YOU! I hate everything you've ever done to me. I can't believe you would treat me like this over and over and over again! I HATE YOU!"

The worst part was, I meant it. I'd thought it numerous times throughout the years, and confessed it to Shawn. I just couldn't deal with her, and now, now I had finally said it out loud, yelled it, and it shut her up. It shut her up so completely I wanted to kill myself when I was done yelling. I put on some nice music for Aryn—after having just tore her Nana a new one—and bawled like a baby the entire drive back to Mom's apartment, pounding my hands on the steering wheel.

We stopped talking. I got phone calls from Cody, too, and I ignored them. That was the end of that relationship. I had crossed a line. I knew it, and I wasn't prepared to face his opinions of me. I didn't listen to any voicemails. I just lived my life as if neither of them existed.

After a while, though, Mom needed me again, and well, I was there. She forgot the terrible things I said to her, because she forgot everything. That was the exact reason I needed to be there with her, because despite my anger, I loved her. I hated what she did to me, I hated that she didn't (or couldn't) think of anyone other than herself, I hated that she had never been the mother a growing girl needed, but I loved her. All the bad didn't take away all the good. That's what kept me coming back. I truly couldn't live without her. I needed her, much in the same way that she needed me. Was it an abusive relationship? Oh yes, and maybe as I grew into an adult, it became abusive on both sides. I don't know my own mistakes as well as she could have relayed them to you.

My point is, I dreaded this moment in our lives for so many reasons. I wanted to make it up to her, to show her that I could be there for her, that I could be the type of person to put aside all our family drama and just be there, just like Grandma Jane had done. Just let it go. I had to let it go, and I had to start helping.

Mom was forgetting what day it was. She was forgetting what time of day it was. She was forgetting what season or even what month it was. Mom was losing her mind, that much was very apparent. I was starting to realize that with her recent disappearances and weird behavior and even weirder stories she was coming back with, she needed the type of help I didn't want to give her but was being forced into. I knew the day was coming that she would have to live in my house.

For now, what I could do was talk to her doctor. After all, he was the person who seemed to know and understand her situation better than anyone.

This was one of the longest days of our lives together.

I left Aryn home with her daddy. I knew better than to bring her into that mess. It wasn't always easy, but it was necessary. I had to let her go. My mother needed me.

When I picked Mom up, she was ready—or nearly so— and she was calm. I can't tell you why she was calm, but she was calm in a disconnected sort of way. I didn't fight with her; I didn't push her to go faster. I helped her get the things she was looking for, her purse, her shoes. I put them on her feet while she sat on her couch rambling at me about this, that, or the other. I listened, I nodded patiently, and I was just *there*. She went at her own pace, and I said the things I was supposed to, only when I knew she was looking for something to be said. She needed reassurance like anyone else might, and that's what I did for her. I was open and

RAISED BY NARCOTICS—The Broken System

honest that I was worried about her, and that I wanted to talk to her doctor alone for a little while. She seemed concerned. Her mind became distracted, and she looked at the windows like something was wrong, like she was looking for an incoming storm. Even though she felt it coming, she couldn't see it.

When we arrived, I felt judgment from the nurses who normally took care of her. These people were becoming attached to her and felt that it was their responsibility to protect her. I admired them for that. Mom needed that from someone. She was always so different around other people than she was with me. She was like a child having a tantrum with their parents, because they know how to manipulate them to get what they wanted. Mom did that to me. She was that child, the same child who was ever so sweet and innocent with every other person that she encountered. Everyone thought she was an angel. It was hard for me not to say something. The resentment built in my heart, with my thoughts going along the lines of *you wouldn't treat her like that if you really knew her*. I kept quiet and let her have her friendships.

Dr. Bennet came in, and the two of them talked about the normal stuff. He asked how she was doing, what was different (if anything), what her symptoms were, and how her meds were. Mom was very short and terse, acting as if everything was fine, when in fact, everything was not fine. I told him I wanted to talk to him alone. He seemed confused. I couldn't do this in front of Mom, though. I had anxiety twisting through my gut at the thought of trying to tell him everything she was going through. But I told him all the same. I told him about the disappearances, her claim to have been diagnosed with cancer and undergoing chemo soon, her inability to tell what day it was, or whether it was day or night just by looking out the window. He sat there quietly, nodding as he listened. It had taken a surprising amount of courage to even talk to this man—a man who was incredibly intimidating to me. He was a doctor, a man who knew things, a man who had seen things, and I was just a dumb girl struggling with her relationship with her mother.

After I finished, he assured me that my mom did not have cancer, and he guided me back into the room with Mom to sit and wait. He said nothing more. Eventually Mom's favorite male nurse came into the room holding a piece of paper. He was young, easy on the eyes, and likely close to my own age. He was sweet, and treated Mom like a child, or an old and frail grandmother. He was compassionate and seemed to genuinely care about her wellbeing. What he held in his hand was a simple test, he said, to see how she was doing.

The test was very basic, something a first grader might be able to ace.

Write your name.
Write today's date.
What month is it?
What's the weather like when you look out the window? Is it sunny? Cold and windy?

On the back there were a few shapes to copy.

RAISED BY NARCOTICS—The Broken System

A circle.

A square.

A simple statement to draw a particular scene.

Mom failed. She failed the simplest test any human can take. She couldn't tell if it was sunny or cloudy, morning or night. She couldn't tell you what day it was, or what season we were in. Her drawings were incoherent squiggles like a preschooler who had just discovered their first pen.

While she concentrated on her test, she asked me questions so that I could help her, and when I had said that I couldn't help her, she looked frustrated. Mom failed.

Shit.

Her favorite, easy-on-the-eyes nurse came back, took the paper, and a few minutes later Dr. Bennet came back in.

I asked, "What do I do now?"

To which he replied, "Find her some type of housing situation."

That's it?

"What about an MRI? Or scan of some kind?"

At that point, he wrote a name on a piece of paper and told us this person might be able to help with housing. Then he let it go.

Mom and I talked easily as we exited his office under the still-sunny sky at the end of summer. She held my hand, I held back my tears. I reassured her that it would be okay, but I knew that it wouldn't. I didn't know what to expect now. I just had to go with the flow, and find the next person who had a different set of knowledge to guide us on the right way to handle what was happening to Mom.

Eventually we made it to the housing office, a small little room where I didn't even dare sit down. I told the administrator why we were there and who had sent us. He looked confused, and well, annoyed. He was in charge of housing options, but he explained that Mom probably wouldn't qualify for any type of assistance. He said this exactly: "Usually family steps in at this point." His hands were clasped at his desk as he sat up straight, glaring directly into my eyes—the biggest hint of my life to have mercy on my mother and take her in. I couldn't explain to him, while she was standing by my side, that it wasn't a good idea. In fact, it might be dangerous.

Just like Dr. Bennet, he handed me another name on a sticky note, and directed me to the financial aid department where she could apply for housing and Medicaid.

We trudged on, stopping at the cafeteria for some lunch. Mom was still calm—not happy, but not upset, as if she could see me trying and wanted to put on a brave face. Looking back, I see what might have really been behind those sad eyes that she tried to mask that day. I believe she may have hit a limit, and no longer wanted to keep trying to be the normal person I expected her to be. Maybe she wanted to run away again. I know that she saw what I saw, however limited her mind was at that moment. She saw that her life was just about to end. Not by means of death, but by handing it over to me as, potentially, her guardian—or being thrown into a nursing home where someone else would be in charge of her. Very real possibilities. Things I had thought of but didn't dare spend too much time thinking about. I absolutely didn't say any of it out loud.

From there, we ended up at the third location with a stack of papers to fill out, and another sticky note with an address where we could see if she qualified for immediate housing assistance.

This process was exhausting. It was just after 5 p.m., and we needed to leave without filling out her papers so that we could make it to the other office before they closed at six. Mom was losing her patience at this point, and she just wanted to go home. I don't know if she knew that she was losing her home soon. To me, it all felt too urgent. I needed a way to get her the help she needed, but so far everyone was just too eager to pass us on to someone else.

We arrived at the fourth location a few minutes before they closed, and almost immediately after relaying her information to someone at the desk (giving away her social security number, her income numbers, and the reasons why this or that), we found out that she did not qualify for anything.

Mom lost it. She had contained her emotions all day—and quite honestly, I was impressed—just to leave literally screaming at me in front of everyone in that office. This felt like a dramatic movie moment in my mind. I stood at the desk begging the clerk to find another way to help me help her. I explained the run around we had been given, and only stopped my explanation to turn and look at my mother. She was wide-eyed and screaming: "I've had enough! I know you don't want me, I know you don't love me! Just throw me away!" Then she stormed out of the building and went to fume in my car. I turned to the receptionist and explained the danger of having her in my home. I spoke in short quick breaths that most definitely conveyed my anxiety that she would have to come live with me. What other choice did I have? I was given that look of pity from the clerk, and they said, "I'm so sorry for what you're going through, but there's nothing we can do. She doesn't qualify." I wanted to scream, too. How did my mother not qualify for anything, even though she was losing everything, including her mind?

We drove home quietly after that. I was too afraid to say anything to her because she could see what I was trying to do, and what was happening. She was losing her mind, but she wasn't so far gone that she couldn't see that her daughter didn't want her living with her.

I was as heartbroken as she was. My whole family was all like me, not wanting to deal with Mom anymore. Everyone wanted to just pass her along, just like I was trying to do. But I was stuck with her.

When we got back to her apartment, I sat down with her stack of papers to fill it all out for her. She stopped me and smiled through her teeth, saying that she would do it herself and put it in the mail first thing in the morning. She said she could tell how exhausted I was, and that I should go home to my baby and get some rest. It had been a long day. She was trying to reassure me.

I was amazed that she was willing to do that, but I think she just wanted to be alone. I left. I trusted her. Still. She

RAISED BY NARCOTICS—The Broken System

said she would do it, so I let her have her way and do it on her own, however much she was losing her grasp on reality. I couldn't be completely sure just how lost she was, so I left her to herself.

There were so many things that I realized that day. In reading it, I'm sure you can guess at most of it.

This was a bad day, but not the worst.

CHAPTER 22

Shelter

I called Jo, sobbing, after Mom got the run-around at Dr. Bennet's office. When I went back to see Mom, she had said that she had filled out the papers and put them in the mail, but my guess is that they ended up in the trash. I could see the fear of being caught in a lie in her eyes, but I didn't know what to do, and I wasn't going to confront her about it. I knew that when she had told herself something, she wasn't going to back down. I didn't want to relive that day again. Mom was a grown woman, capable of making her own decisions, and I needed to let her—or so I kept telling myself. In reality, I just didn't want to fight with her anymore.

The conversation with Jo, and later Ray, came about because I second-guessed how capable Mom really was when it came to making her own decisions. Jo sat with me while I had a panic attack, pacing my kitchen and not knowing what to do. She gave me the number for their family lawyer to talk about options for taking over guardianship of my own mother. Afterwards, I somehow ended up having a very extensive conversation with Ray in his kitchen. While Aryn played with toys and ran around our feet, I tried to wrap my head around being a mother to my own mother. He reassured me that I was doing everything I could. I had never felt so connected to this man in all the time I had known him—not until this very moment where he literally grabbed my hand and reassured me that not wanting to bring my mother into my home wasn't a bad thing.

That was one of the only moments where I felt like I had parents to lean on for help and guidance in an impossible situation. They both, in their different ways, helped me understand what was really happening to her, and what I could realistically do for her in that situation. Becoming her guardian would be a huge responsibility and it would put a lot of strain on my family, but it might have to be done. I felt that I was running out of options, so all I could do was just sit and take it a day at a time.

A few days later, I received a call from Mom on her fiftieth birthday. She was returning my attempt to call and wish her a happy day. I would have bought a cake so that Aryn and I could celebrate Nana's big five-zero, but Mom was not home. She said she was in the canyon, having the time of her life. Steve had come back to get her, and he had taken her on a little vacation. She warned me that she might lose service, but before she did I promised that next time she was home I would pick her up and make her a cake. She was so excited for that, and honestly, so was I. We needed something normal, but Mom had left again with Steve, and I wasn't sure how long that would last, or who was going to pay for her apartment. She wasn't lost this time, so that was one positive out of the situation, but she wasn't doing smart things. She was acting like a teenager, running away with her new love, leaving behind her responsibilities because it was more fun that way. Mom was trying to have fun—and I wanted to let her do that before I either put her in a nursing home, or took ownership of her every action and brought her into mine.

Shawn and I didn't have a lot of money to deal with either situation, but I knew I had my in-laws for help if I really needed it. I just really hated asking, after everything we had taken from them already to get a leg up in life. Shawn felt entitled to it because he was their son, and that made sense to me, but I was not their daughter and I was struggling with how to present myself to them so that they didn't think all I wanted was their money. Money helps, but I had pride—a lot of it—and this wasn't their problem. It was mine.

About a week after Mom's birthday, I got a call at 11:30 p.m. I was plugging in my phone to charge for the night on my bedside table when she called me in a panic. I could hardly understand what she was saying, but she was asking me to come and get her. She was bawling, and scared. She said that she was alone and had locked the door.

What have you done now, Mom?

I tried to have her slow down, and I told her I would come get her if I needed to. She was in Delta, though,

RAISED BY NARCOTICS—Shelter

roughly three hours' drive away from my home. Making that kind of trip in the middle of the night was not necessarily safe, but I would do it for her. I was already thinking of how to get down there and find a hotel for us when she said, "Oh, they're here."

"Who's there, Mom?" I asked, confused.

"The shelter. I called the shelter to come pick me up. I'm not safe here, don't worry about me, they're here to get me."

Oh, God was I confused.

"I need to go," she said.

"Call me in the morning, please, Mom," I begged.

Jesus Christ, this was never going to get any easier, was it?

I battled every single day with what to do about this situation. On one hand, she had made her way to a shelter. On the other hand, her entire life was hours away from Delta—her pills, her things, her family—and none of us knew what to do.

What I knew about Mom was that she wanted her independence. Immediately, the women's shelter where she ended up had given her a room to herself, one that locked, with a mini-fridge to keep some food. From what she told me, it sounded like a small dorm, but she still didn't have everything she needed. And yet, she said she wanted to handle her life all on her own.

Honestly, she sounded happy. She said she had made friends there, very quickly, and had a little home away from home. It didn't sound like she wanted to leave. We absolutely should have gone to pick her up—but if I did, she would end up living with me, end of story, and I still wasn't prepared. I sat on the thought for longer than I should have.

In November, I found myself on my friend Meghan's couch while she packed up her clothes to move out of state. She said that because she was getting rid of so many things, I could take whatever I wanted to send to Mom. I was grateful, both for the clothes she was donating to my poor sad Mom, and also for the listening ear she gave me as I sat trying to explain what was happening.

I took those clothes, bought a few boxes of cereal, some gloves, and a hat and a scarf. I also got a pillow because she had requested it, as well as some little stationery and stamps so she could write letters and send them to us. I was surprised by that last part—I guess Mom was finding some fun in it all. I boxed it all up, put her name on it, and sent it on its way. It arrived in a few days, and Mom was completely elated. She called me so happy she was crying, but that was just Mom. Her emotions ran deep, and she felt everything very intensely. Every emotion was overwhelming.

Unfortunately, things were still not great—she was in a shelter with strangers, and without proper medical care. I wasn't sure what she was doing to take care of herself and her illness, and she didn't ask if I would send her anything or come get her. What she did call and ask for was money, but I had already decided on a hard and fast rule to not send any. I would send her anything else she needed, but not money. Who knew what she would spend it on, or where it would go? I knew she wouldn't buy what she really needed, so I did it to protect her. Then, she caught me with a loophole to my plan and told me she just needed $17 to get a copy of her birth certificate. Hmm, well, that changed everything, didn't it? Should I just send the $17 for a birth certificate? Or should I find a way to go take her to get it myself? There was also the problem of the drive down there—it was so long, and I wasn't prepared to face her. The drive itself wasn't all that difficult. I grew up taking road trips that were much longer than that, and I loved being in the car. Nevertheless, this was the excuse I gave to her because I knew the minute I showed up, it would be to have her pack what little she had and bring her to my home. There were a growing number of reasons why I still couldn't (and wouldn't) do that.

So, $17 for a birth certificate so she could start getting her life together again and be an adult? Sure, why the hell not. I could find a way to wire the money, and I did my best to reassure her that I would call her back and figure it out, leaving it on my growing list of "to-do for Mom."

I never had the chance to send the money. I sat on my hands for a while before actually doing anything about it. I guess I was waiting to hear back from her on whether or not it was still relevant. She couldn't give me a reason about why she needed it in the first place, so . . . I let it slip.

Christmas came and went. It was one of the worst Christmases I had ever had. All the normal traditions that I used to keep myself busy and neglect the situation with my mother were overshadowed by guilt and depression. I remember hiding behind my camera, just walking around like a zombie as Shawn's family opened presents and ate the wonderful Christmas brunch Jo made every year, while we all still wore our pajamas. Aryn thought it was so much fun. She was four now, nearly five come the spring, and everything was magical for her.

I took hundreds of photos to preoccupy myself and keep myself from saying too much to the people around me. There was one point, while I sat eating the traditional omelet loaded with veggies and cheese, where I completely broke down. I had to stand up as fast as I could and go to the bathroom to cry. I stood in front of the mirror and asked myself what the hell I was doing. Mom was out there all alone on Christmas day. Had my life been anything like a Hollywood tearjerker, I would have run to my car, still in my Christmas PJs, and driven all the way down to her and brought her home. From there the movie would end with hugs, laughter, and the present I had hidden under the tree just for her, and everything would somehow work out in the end. But instead I stood there, beating myself up that I wasn't that person, because I was very literally afraid of my mother and having her ruin the life I had created for myself. I suddenly felt sick.

The stress was catching up to me. One of my only friends was moving two states away, my mother was in a women's shelter three hours from home doing God knows what, Cody wasn't speaking to me, I still couldn't figure out my life—although things were stable for once. Obviously, I'm not talking about my emotions—those were a wreck—but financially and otherwise, I guess... That was just it: I second guessed all my decisions. I doubted whether I was really cut out for the life I was trying to create for myself and my little family. I sat watching Shawn's siblings laugh and play with toys, even though they were all adults. The tradition was to buy some hot toy of the year and we all take turns playing with it. I was jealous, I was hurting. I wanted to run screaming from the room. Instead, I pointed my camera at my little girl and I caught as much of the magic in the holiday through her perspective as I could, and when the day was over, I went back to our home, only two blocks away, and slept it all off.

That day was the beginning of the depression that would haunt me for the next several years, and my dilemma with Mom was far from over yet. I had no idea what was to come.

CHAPTER 23

I'm Late

The holidays are a busy time of year for nearly every family in this country. But for us, it has special meaning beyond just making it through the constant commercialism. We celebrate our wedding anniversary on January 4th, so it's a rush of activity, and then it just stops. This year was no different, and as we rang in 2012, and then celebrated our anniversary with a little night out on the town, I had the realization that I had missed my period.

At this point it had been one year since I had found my father. We no longer spoke; it was just too hard to try to put together a relationship that was broken years before it ever started. I couldn't maintain it or even think about it. It was hard remembering what had happened, and how fast I had lost the thing I never really had to begin with—but I had bigger fish to fry, so to speak.

I realized I had missed my period the day after our anniversary, and then it still didn't show up. You're wondering about this, now aren't you? An oops baby?

RAISED BY NARCOTICS—I'm Late

Nope. A very intentional baby. But at such a time? Was I an idiot? Probably.

A few months earlier, after Shawn had found his stable job and our benefits were kicking in, I sat scrapbooking some baby pictures of Aryn. I was trying to catch up on my albums that I had neglected and filling my mind with my little girl instead of what Mom was going through. Pictures were so important to me. I saw her chubby little baby face and decided that I wasn't done having babies. I wanted one more. I loved the feeling of being a mom, even if I wasn't perfect at it, and it just made sense. Life wasn't going to get any more stable than this. We had both graduated, we already had one little bundle of joy that I was staying at home with, and I wanted another shot at being a new mom. I wanted the big belly and the little fluttery kicks of my unborn child. I wanted the little newborn in my arms and the chance to stay home and do it right. I wanted to breastfeed, I wanted the healthy bonding at the hospital, because Aryn had been taken away so fast after her lung collapsed. I simply wanted to see if I could do it and enjoy it a second time. This time I would know what I was doing and do it right.

Aryn had a rough start to her life, much the same way I did. That's funny to reflect on—I don't think I had put those two pieces of life together until now. We share similar birth stories, and I now have a new way to look at my connection to the strong little girl I'm raising.

When I was born, my lungs were full of fluid. Mom told me that it took the doctors nearly thirty minutes to get me to breathe. She remembered the clock saying 2:08 a.m., but because of my difficult entrance into the world, my birth certificate reads 2:32 a.m. I had tubes shoved into my nose, and I suffered a broken nose because of it. I still have a bump on the bridge of my nose to prove it. It's the only evidence I have that what she said really happened. They thought I was going to die. Another accident in my life, right at the very beginning. One broken nose later, and here I am with an entire story to tell.

Aryn's situation was not nearly as life threatening as mine, thanks to new technology and a very caring pediatrician. My OBGYN, however, was not as caring. He was never really interested in what was happening to me during my pregnancy. He didn't even show up to help deliver her until ten minutes before she arrived. Maybe this is hindsight. He was older, much older, and I was a very naïve twenty-year-old girl not knowing what to do or what was normal.

My OB told me, at 41-weeks pregnant, that I should be induced into labor. At 41-weeks pregnant, it took some serious convincing to get my doctor to listen to me. Okay, that last sentence doesn't even make sense to me, so let me explain the best way I can. My doctor, the one who was supposed to help me deliver this child into the world, told me that I should be induced at 41 weeks. That was the birth plan. Maybe he himself was losing his mind like my mother was, because he didn't remember any of this, and it was impossible to get anyone to listen to me. The nurses I called in Labor and Delivery acted like they had no clue what was

RAISED BY NARCOTICS—I'm Late

going on. Aryn wasn't coming out. No signs whatsoever of labor. I was huge and stressed, and miserable, and my doctor wouldn't listen to me even when it was his advice I was given and attempting to express. I took myself into Labor and Delivery at 41 weeks and told the staff there that I was told I was to be induced. They all gave me confused looks, the same looks I imagine they gave me on the phone when I called earlier that day, and finally they decided to call up my doctor. To my surprise, they didn't send me home. To their surprise, my daughter was born at nine pounds two ounces, and because of her size, which my doctor had not bothered to monitor, her right lung collapsed as she entered the world. Many years later I would find out that there was a possibility that I did, in fact, have gestational diabetes during this pregnancy. I will come back to this a little later.

Immediately the nurses grabbed her from the doctor, and I barely had a chance to catch a glimpse of her little feet. She wasn't crying. She couldn't. They cleaned her off quickly, wrapped her in a blanket, put a little hat on her head, as was customary, and put her in my arms. She couldn't cry, she couldn't breathe. For all of two seconds I held my first child in my arms, looking down at her as our worlds shifted together. She tried, desperately, to make her voice reach my ears, but all that came out was a whimper. A breathy silence. Something was wrong with my baby.

The nurses took her from my arms immediately, put her in the little plastic bassinet, and rushed her out of the room. Shawn glanced at me, worried for his new baby girl and asked me "Are you okay if I go with her?" and I nodded. That's all I could do, and he left me.

I stayed where I was, literally paralyzed from having an epidural. I had just given birth to my first child and I didn't even know what proper contractions felt like—all I knew was that my legs felt like Jell-O.

Because of her size, she had obviously torn me up on her way out. The doctor quickly stitched me up while I stared at the ceiling, not knowing what to think. I think the doctor made some weird joke because I remember him laughing, and the one nurse who was left in the room with us to clean up the mess laughed with him. My family wasn't in the room because I had wanted it all to be private. I wanted the birth of my daughter to be my experience. Not theirs. So they waited in the lobby, not knowing what was happening. As soon as my doctor was finished with the stitches, and the nurse was finished cleaning my blood off the floor, they left my room. I lay in my hospital bed alone. Completely alone.

I had just given birth to a human being. She existed now outside of me, when these past 41 weeks she had only existed as a part of me. Now, I felt empty, and more alone then I had ever been. I tried to remember her little face when they had placed her in my arms for all of two seconds, but I couldn't. I didn't know what her hair looked like because of the stupid little hat on her head. I didn't know what she looked like, if she had my nose or Shawn's. And in that moment, I detached. I had given birth, but my baby was gone. Was she really even mine? Was I really even a

RAISED BY NARCOTICS—I'm Late

mother? I was just a girl, stuck in a hospital bed. Life was happening without me. Already, she didn't need me.

I began to float through the next several hours. Shawn eventually came in, and had photos to show me, and good news. They had inflated her lung, and as he showed me the three photos he had taken of her, I noticed that her head was under what looked to me like a fish bowl— it was an oxygen bubble. Her eyes were squinted almost shut, and it sort of made her look Asian. Not like my baby, although she did have dark hair just like me, but I kept staring at her waiting for the moment that it would register that this child was mine, that I was a mom now.

People started coming in, while my daughter laid in the NICU under her bubble like a fish, and I lay in a bed apart from her, blood pooling under my ass and the blankets that covered me. More uncomfortable things no one tells you about having a baby. You'll lie in bed seemingly bleeding to death, but it's normal, and while you can feel it seeping out of your body, people will want to lean over you and hug you and wish you congratulations. Later on you'll have to stand up with that blood sloshing around in your weird netted underwear, having nurses help you sit on a toilet with the door wide open, your legs spread wide and use a little spray bottle to spray water all over yourself to clean the blood off. Then they'll help you shove ice packs and giant pads inside your amazing netted underwear and pull it up for you because your hands are busy holding yourself upright because your legs are still jelly.

After all of that, they put me into a wheelchair, and finally, five hours later, wheeled me in to see my daughter for the second time since giving birth to her. The first real time I would get to see her, touch her skin, and wish I could just hold onto her like a normal mother.

What came next were several visits like that one. She was born in the afternoon just after 4:00—4:20 p.m., actually. So, after 9:00 when I finally saw her again, I was able to come back to my hospital bed and pretend that it had never happened and fall asleep. Sleep without my child next to me, or cradled inside of me, safely kicking and hiccupping in her usual manner. Not that night. That night her normal kicks and wiggles didn't keep me awake, and the drugs I was on put me fast asleep. Percocet. Sleeping as if nothing had ever happened.

I forgot the day and forgot what was happening to my baby girl all the through the night, as she fought through the pain of air bubbles in her chest dissipating slowly. What was she feeling? Did she feel the pain of being poked in the chest with a tube to inflate the lung that had collapsed? I didn't want to consider it. Whatever I woke up to, it wasn't up to me. I was just coasting and sleeping a long sleep because it was all that I could do.

The morning after, I went to visit her and put my foot down, now that my legs weren't jelly. I had started to manage my bleeding vagina on my own, and I demanded that I get to be her mother. I should be the one to change her diaper and feed her. Of course, they had put her on formula through the night while I was knocked out on

RAISED BY NARCOTICS — I'm Late

heavy drugs due to the pain that they told me I would have but had never had a chance to feel. A decision I hadn't made. Or had I? I couldn't remember.

Twenty-four hours after her ordeal, she was released from the NICU and rolled into my bedroom. Shawn had been with her through most of it, not getting much of a chance to sleep and splitting his time between the two of us. Together we were able to watch her get her first bath that afternoon. They put a little pink bow in her hair, and little white cotton shirt with mittens over her hands with the logo of the hospital printed on the front, then wrapped her in a thin little blanket with blue and pink baby feet covering it.

Now, she was in my room. Now, I got to be a mother. Now . . . I didn't know what to do next. How did I feed her? How did I know that she needed a diaper change? Did I try to breast feed? My nipples hurt a little bit. Why? I didn't have answers. One of my nurses came in and tried to talk me through it.

"It's going to be hard, because she's already used to the bottle nipple, and not yours, but here," she said holding my breast in her hand while I cradled my baby under it, shoving it quickly into her mouth, and Aryn, finally finding her voice, screaming at the top of her newly inflated lungs.

I wanted to be a mother, the kind that breastfed her child, normally, naturally. Aryn and I tried every hour, but she just grew hungrier and angrier. She would suck for a few seconds and let go, screaming at me. I was agitated. Was this what being a mother was? I just wanted her to stop screaming at me. I needed her to stop. I couldn't love her if she kept screaming. I broke down. I sobbed and told Shawn, feeling like a failure, that I couldn't do it. We hadn't even left the hospital yet, and I couldn't do it. Had I even really tried? This was too hard. She didn't want me, she just wanted her bottle, and I wanted to put her down, go to sleep and wake up with it having only been a terrible nightmare. But it wasn't.

As soon as I made that decision to just give her a bottle—finally, finally, I became a mother. I hated myself for the decision, but it was the best one. For both of us. She stopped screaming, and I held her in my arms, the way I had imagined myself doing all through my pregnancy. I held her tiny fingers while she ate and fluttered her eyes, and in that moment, she became my daughter. However, I was still detached from her in a way I couldn't realize until several years later when I had the chance to try again.

Aryn was four now, and it made sense to give her someone to play with, and a new member of our family to love. Aryn and Shawn were becoming my family, a word that I struggled to find meaning in, until I found them and looked into their faces and realized they were mine. I was settled, and I wanted to do it again. What I didn't realize was how fast it would happen. Aryn took six months to conceive, but I had been on the pill. Now I had an IUD and my doctor, a new one at the clinic down the street from the house we bought from Shawn's parents, had told me that once it was out, I could get pregnant immediately. It was totally unlike other contraceptives that leave lingering hormones which make it harder to get pregnant quickly.

RAISED BY NARCOTICS—I'm Late

I just didn't realize how fertile I was. I had the IUD removed at the end of November 2011, and I must have gotten pregnant right after my very first period after having it out. Literally within days. It explained everything. The "flu" I had gotten after trying to help Meghan pack up and move mid-December. The influx of emotion and sickness on Christmas Day. Everything made sense.

I took a pregnancy test January 5th and confirmed it. I told Shawn in a cutesy way, baking sugar cookies that spelled it out and surprising him when he came home from work. I put Aryn's little hand on my belly to show her she was going to be a big sister. It was something we had talked about before, and she was so excited. She was in that phase of asking for a little sister constantly, and who knows, maybe it was her four-year-old persuasion that finally made me cave.

On January 6th, 2012, I called the girls on Shawn's side of the family over, including his grandma who was in town, to tell them the good news. They were all properly excited for me, said congrats, high fived the new big sister, ate a cookie, and left. My night became empty, because of course there had been someone who hadn't been there, and I struggled with the fact that she had been the very first person I had told when I found out about Aryn. She had supported me and given me the excitement I needed to feel great about my decision. She gave me the courage to move forward despite how young I was.

My mom. Mom loved babies. She would be the one person who would have been the most excited to welcome another grandchild—her fourth—but she was still in the shelter, and I still didn't know what to do. I wondered if I was making a mistake expanding my family and shutting out my own mother.

I thought I would have time to sort out what to do about her situation first, and then bring this life into the world and give us all some happiness—but it all happened at once, because that's life. Life just happens all at once. The good, and the bad.

That night when the girls left my house, I sat staring out the big window in my living room, the one that reminded me of Grandma Jane's big window at her house on Nebo Drive. I sat with the phone in my hand, debating how to tell Mom. I would call, of course, but how would she react? Would she be happy? Would she be mad that she wasn't here? I was so lost. What if she didn't answer? Should I just keep calling? Should I finally go get her and bring her into my home and settle everything, so my family could all be safe and happy? I could bring Mom back and set up a nursery in my bedroom. The baby would have to stay in there for a few months anyways. I could take Mom to help me pick out a new bassinet, since she was so upset when I got rid of the last one. If the baby was a girl, she could share a room with Aryn, and maybe we could finish one of the rooms in the basement for Mom?

So many thoughts and plans and what ifs.

I could make it work regardless, but right now I had to call Mom. If she found out from anyone else, she would be devastated.

RAISED BY NARCOTICS—I'm Late

She didn't answer her phone. *Oh shit.* I had to hurry and decide if I was going to leave it in a message. Would she be offended that I didn't wait to hear her voice? I never did anything right, and it wouldn't matter however I did it, so I did.

"Hey, Mom, so I, uh, have some good news!" I said, trying to sound as cheerful as I possibly could. "I'm pregnant! I found out yesterday, Aryn's going to be a big sister." Yeah, there you go, she can't get mad at sweet little Aryn. "Call me back when you get this please, I love you, and I hope you're doing okay." And that was it, I hung up.

That was a Friday night. Mom didn't call me back all weekend, and I was terrified that I had offended her so badly she just couldn't speak to me. I had abandoned her and left her for dead, even if she had gotten herself into that situation. I expected her to be an adult and get herself out of it, but in her eyes, it was my fault that she wasn't safe and happy, and now I was replacing her with more babies to take care of and going to forget her entirely.

The anxiety I felt was awful.

Come Monday, as I sat on the couch eating Pop-Tarts and watching TV, waiting for my alarm to pick up Aryn from preschool to go off, my phone rang. It was Mom.

"Hey, Mom," I said apprehensively. "What's up?"

"Oh, Alyse, I have the best news!" The weight in my heart lifted at her words. She was happy.

"Oh yeah, Mom what's that?" I asked, grinning now. It was going to be a good day.

"My daughter is going to have a baby!" she exclaimed, and I laughed.

We talked for only a minute or two, and of course Mom started crying. While she was talking excitedly about her new grandbaby, I heard the alarm on my phone go off in my ear. It was time to pick up Aryn. I pulled it away and shut it off quickly, giving Mom a few more minutes to talk about it, and tell her how happy I was that she called me back. I told her that it meant the world to me that she was excited, but eventually I had to cut the conversation off.

"Mom, I have to go pick up Aryn from school. Can I call you back later?"

"Yes, of course. Alyse, I love you so much! I'm just so happy!"

"I'm so happy too Mom, I love you too. See you later."

"See you later, CeCe," she said, tugging at my heart a little more. She used the nickname she had given me to say goodbye. She had said "see you later," because goodbye was too permanent, and Mom didn't like that. She would never let you get away with saying goodbye. She always corrected you with a "see you later."

Those were the last words I ever heard her speak.

CHAPTER 24

The End

More than two weeks had passed. I was going through the motions and feeling both incredibly sick with my new baby growing inside of me, and feeling the weight of the depression and unsettled questions that loomed over me every single day.

It was mid-winter, the holidays were over, the excitement was done, and life went on like normal. Even though Mom was in the shelter, we both still let time lapse between us without making much of an effort to reach out to each other. I still held onto all the buzzing questions about what to do with her, but life was marching forward, and who knew, maybe she had plans of her own. Maybe she was happy being homeless. She wasn't making much effort to come back this time, and she wasn't asking anyone for more help. I still sent food to her, and basic things like shampoo and soap, but otherwise, we were falling into a weird routine. Could you even have a routine being homeless like that? When I had spoken to her in the weeks before

Christmas, she had seemed happy to have her shelter friends, and people she could connect with. Maybe that's what she needed. I couldn't really know.

It was now January 23, 2012. I was about six weeks pregnant. I hadn't even had my first official doctor appointment to confirm the pregnancy and see my little bean on the screen through an ultrasound. But I very much felt pregnant, and I didn't need a doctor to confirm it, because I was sick and exhausted, and the further the pregnancy went on, the more severe my symptoms became. Mostly, I just really couldn't keep my eyes open.

It was a Monday, so Aryn had school, and I continued to take it easy. I planned a little activity that she and I could do together after school, because I was starting to feel guilty that I wasn't being much of a mom these days. She was getting bored, and though she enjoyed playing alone or with the little crafts I bought for her, it didn't stop me from feeling like I needed to be more active and present.

We sat at the kitchen table making her craft when my phone rang, a shrill car-horn ringtone that I had assigned to only one person—Cody.

He never called me, and when he did it was usually to yell at me for offending Mom again. But I hadn't spoken to her since telling her about the baby, so it couldn't possibly be that. I debated letting it go to voicemail, but at the last minute I picked up.

It was about Mom—I had been right about that—but she was being life-flighted to a nearby hospital.

What a convenient way for her to come home.

RAISED BY NARCOTICS — The End

Fight or flight kicked in pretty fast as he spoke to me, and my mind rattled off what I was supposed to do next.

Find a babysitter.

Was Mom dying?

What happened?

"Aryn get your shoes on. No, we have to wait to finish daddy's gift."

What about dinner?

Should I pack a snack?

Where are my shoes?

Is it safe to drive like this?

I can barely keep my eyes open.

Shit, what's happening?!

Where's my coat?

I was twenty-five. I had one child, and another on the way. We were stable, for the most part, and finally living a somewhat normal life for the first time ever in my entire life.

Am I about to watch my mother die?

What about everything I didn't get a chance to do for her? I still need to help her figure out her situation. What happened to her apartment? I had already grabbed anything I had wanted out of it months earlier, and there was nothing in it of any value to me. Had she already lost it? Had her stuff been taken? Dammit, I needed to figure this stuff out. My brain was exhausted.

Somehow, I found a friend who could take Aryn for a sleepover. I told Shawn what was happening as I drove to the hospital.

When I arrived, the first thing Cody did was wrap me up in his arms. It was so startling that I burst into tears. Everything else floated into the past now, never to be seen again. A turning point in both our lives. We were about to lose our mother, and that was all that mattered anymore.

He explained to me that she'd had a stroke. Just like Teresa. She had been in her room, in her bed, and someone at the shelter had found her that way after knocking on her door.

She was dying the exact same way Teresa did. The lupus had finally taken her brain, or so I assumed.

Shawn arrived after leaving work early. The doctors eventually came in. I had never met this doctor before, but he was kind and gentle with what he said. He showed me brain scans, so I could see the damage to my mother's brain. He said he could operate, but because of where the stroke had happened, she would be left without any ability to speak for herself or use her arms. She would be paralyzed, *if* she survived the surgery at all, and in her condition her chances were quite low.

For years Mom had told us that she did not want to live a life where she was a vegetable. I don't think many people do—where's the quality in that? I agreed with her, and in facing that situation, I didn't second guess it. Neither did Cody. We both agreed, because after all she had been through, we weren't about to make her go through that too.

Her time was done, her life . . . over. She already didn't have quality of life, what good would it do now to keep her

RAISED BY NARCOTICS—The End

locked up in a nursing home unable to even feed herself or speak her thoughts?

So, now we waited. We waited for the inevitable end, and I waited to feel anything about what was happening. I was in shock.

Mom was dying.

Mom was going to die.

Mom would never wake up again.

This was the end. In a few days we would have a funeral. We would bury her body in the ground. I would see her for the last time before we closed the casket on her cold body, and I would never be burdened by her situation in life, or her emotional abuse ever again.

I rattled off the situation like that in my mind. I felt crazy for doing so. I wanted to feel reality, but I couldn't.

I sat in the room next to Mom. I joked with my family, Cody, Mandy, Shawn, and Aunt Sylvia. We gathered around her to talk about her, Teresa, and Grandma Jane. None of us cried while we surrounded her. None of us fought about whether to tell anyone else about it. We all silently agreed that we would wait. I wasn't going to allow anyone to come into this moment and take away the last moments I had with my mother.

Shortly after the doctor came in to explain Mom's situation, a nurse came in and took away all of Mom's cords—the things keeping her breathing and alive. I sat with her, trying to hold her hand, gently rubbing her arm, petting her hair, and staring at her. Absorbing the last of the life she had, because soon, it would be over. How soon though?

I jokingly said, "Geez, Mom, you're taking your sweet time, aren't you?" but that was after a few hours. It was past midnight, and everyone was getting restless.

I hadn't eaten in several hours. I was sick, hungry, exhausted. I was fighting against sleep while my muscles shook from the chill in the sterile hospital room. Eventually everyone just sat by her side quietly, and we all waited.

Waited.

Waited.

It began to snow outside. I could see out the window from my chair next to her bed. No one wanted to take the chair from the pregnant woman losing her mother, but I couldn't sit there anymore, despite the hour—now 3 a.m. I gave it up and insisted that Shawn take it so he could sleep. I would need him to get me through tomorrow, and I couldn't sleep in this room. I couldn't close my eyes to my dying mother, so I stood by the window instead, watching the slow and gentle cascades of snow falling onto the grass below.

Time stood still, and that's when it hit me. This was the end. Anything I had been planning to do, I would never have the chance to do now. I struggled with guilt for feeling relief, and also the deep sorrow of losing my mother. She was still important to me, and all I wanted was to shake her awake. I wanted to slap her and pour water on her face the way she had done to Teresa eight years ago.

Eight years.

RAISED BY NARCOTICS—The End

Four years for Grandma Jane.

Now Mom.

The goddamn curse.

The New Year had just started, and Mom was now here lying on her deathbed, waiting for her last breath. I was almost angry at her, as if she had done it on purpose. This was never going to end. Who was going to come next?

I sat back down in one of the folding chairs and emailed Meghan from my iPhone. I didn't expect a response, but apparently, she's a night owl. I got a ding only a few minutes later with her condolences and wishes that she could be with me. She talked with me through the night and helped me wrap my head around what was happening.

Eventually, about 5 a.m., I left the hospital in search of sleep in my own bed. Mom was still alive, and I was having a really hard time waiting it out. Cody and his wife had gone to take his girls to her parents' house for the night and take a shower. Surely if he did that, and still had time to come back, I could go and get an hour or so of rest, take a shower, and come back in the light of day with a fresh head and some food in my stomach.

Shawn drove me home on empty streets. Nothing felt real. It was like living inside of a dream. Cliché, I know, but there's a reason that people say that. I could see the stars, the same stars I had found solace in time and time again throughout my life. Somehow the night sky comforted me. It was quiet and peaceful. It reminded me that death, however permanent, wasn't permanent. We were all stardust, right? We were all connected, here, there, or anywhere.

Mom would die.

Soon.

I pushed these thoughts out of my head. I let the exhaustion hit me. I let myself go. At home I took off my clothes, put on pajamas, and put my favorite sweater into the washing machine—because I knew one thing, I would need comfort when I woke up. I set an alarm for myself so that I would wake up, and hopefully not to the sound of my phone ringing and Cody telling me it had already happened. I knew that was a possibility, but after dealing with this twice before, I didn't know if it really mattered. What I suspected was that it would matter to Cody, and somehow it did matter to me. I would not be happy with myself if after finally caving to my desperate need for rest and normalcy, I missed watching her pass on, as I had missed the other two for my own selfish needs. I didn't sleep well that night—or morning, rather. I finally got myself out of bed again and put myself into the shower, letting the hot water wash over me. I don't know how long I stood in there. Too long, and suddenly remembered that I had never put my favorite sweater into the dryer. I needed it. I yelled at Shawn to do it for me, but I felt the urgency set in that it would take me at least thirty minutes to drive to the hospital again, and I needed to get out of the shower. I needed to be put together, but I wouldn't do my makeup, because I had made that mistake the day before already, and the nurse told me that I looked like a mess. She actually said that to my face.

RAISED BY NARCOTICS — The End

Well, no shit, I thought. *My mother is dying in the next room. I don't believe you would look like a fucking super model with all her shit together. Of course I'm a mess, and mascara running down my face is the last thing I'm worried about!*

So, no make up for me. I didn't need my looks on display while I watched my mother die, but I did need that damn sweater. I paced my home waiting for it to dry.

Unfortunately, it would have to wait. I had to go. I had to hurry. How much longer would Mom really hold on? I had been selfish with my time already.

I thought of Mom lying in her hospital bed in the ICU. Did she feel anything? Did she know anyone was there? Did she hear me? Could she feel me when I had touched her arm, or brushed her hair with my hand? I couldn't imagine she felt any pain. That was the one thing I knew was gone, because I knew the feeling of not feeling the pain you were supposed to feel.

I had Shawn grab me one of his fleece sweaters. I felt fat and ugly, my hair not done, and pulled into a bun behind my head. Jeans, sweater, and death written all over my face. This would have to do.

I drove quickly. Faster then I should have. I had an incredible amount of road rage, pissing off the drivers around me, as I yelled words they couldn't hear. I told them get out of my fucking way, my mother is dying, and I need to be there!

If it had really been that much of an emergency, why hadn't I stayed?

And then my phone rang. No. No, not now. I sped faster, and finally got to the entrance of the hospital parking garage. My phone rang again. I parked, nearly hitting the large cement pillar holding the whole structure together.

I answered my phone: "I'm here, just come downstairs, I'm here!" I practically yelled into the phone.

"Alyse . . ."

"No. Don't you dare tell me!" I sounded just like Mom. Don't you dare. How dare you tell me she's already gone. And I hung up on him.

Somehow, we made it up the elevators, and at the top Cody was waiting for me. He reached out and wrapped me up in his arms. She was gone.

I missed her last breath by ten minutes, her body still warm in her death bed, the life sucked out of her, her mouth gaping open, her arms resting at her side with a clean white sheet pulled up over her.

I burst into tears, again. The finality of her death pierced me in such a way that I thought I would die with her. We would never have a chance to make things right between us.

It was over.

The nurses and Cody let me sit with her before they took her body away. I don't know how long I was there, but I remember exactly what I was thinking. I held onto her hand, squeezing her still warm fingers, rubbing the still warm flesh of her arm with my other hand. I held onto that warmth for dear life. I needed to remember this moment. I absorbed it. I breathed it in. I took in every single detail of

RAISED BY NARCOTICS—The End

my mother's body and mentally captured what her warmth felt like. In only a few hours she wouldn't be warm anymore, and by the time I saw her next she would be quite hard, and leathery, like a dead cow. I remembered Teresa, and what she felt like eight years before. I remembered Grandma Jane and the quick touch to her hands as she lay in her casket four years before, before quickly pulling away because it had been a mistake to do that again. I wouldn't touch my mother after this moment. No more too-long hugs. No more long goodbyes, holding hands in her doorway wishing she would just let me go. Now, she had let me go, and I couldn't let her go. All the things we didn't get to do together. All the moments we never got to have. The baby that would never know its Nana.

It was all gone now.

January 24, 2012: Mom was dead.

CHAPTER 25

Floating

Mom died sometime just before or just after 11 a.m. The funny thing about death is that for those who are left living, things don't really change. This was not my first rodeo, obviously, but now all three of them were gone. Somehow it was different. It was like a dim light that was flickering had finally burned out. Everything went dark, and I started floating through my actions.

We picked up Aryn from my friend's house. I don't know what I said to them, but Mom had just barely died. I only remember how they looked at me, which was a lot of pity and concern, and then I walked away. I was really hungry, and we all wanted lunch. I had yet to explain to Aryn that Nana was dead. I hadn't even thought about it.

I just wanted something normal, so we drove to the donut shop for donuts and chocolate milk. I laughed out loud as we sat in the drive-thru waiting for them. Mom had just died, and I was buying donuts. 'Mkay . . . why not?

RAISED BY NARCOTICS—Floating

The details of planning a funeral are boring. How I waited at the funeral home for my brother to show up, staring out the window from the place that I knew like the back of my hand. I knew which doors led to the caskets. I knew which doors led to the dead people in the basement. I watched as the car that carried my mother's body drove up and around the building, and I stared at my little red Prius as my brother drove up in his lifted forest-green Jeep, parking in the space next to mine in the very empty parking lot. I stared at the pamphlets sitting strategically on the coffee tables that sat in front of the couches, trying to sell me on the ways I could try to keep my loved one's memory alive.

Did I want to keep her memory alive?

I was numb. This was a routine. I knew I would write the obituary. I knew I would pick out photos for the slideshow. I knew I would print photos to display and go to Carrie's floral shop next door to pick out flowers. I knew I would pick out the cheapest casket we could find, and I knew my brother would joke about his own funeral, because he was just like Mom, and Mom had done the same thing at both Teresa's and Grandma Jane's funeral preparations. I knew that I would be expected to stand up and say something in front of people I hated and who had no love or respect for the woman who had just died. I knew that I would have to tell people—and I couldn't do it. I asked Aunt Sylvia, and she was very eager to help.

When you're grieving, you need busy work, and it all came crashing down on me—and yet I thrived. But the one thing I just couldn't do was talk to people. I didn't want to attend a funeral where everyone would be looking at me. I knew I wouldn't stand in a line proceeding Mom's casket. I knew I wouldn't look at her. I knew I wouldn't touch her cold, hard, leathery flesh. I knew I wouldn't be doing her makeup or her hair. I knew I would have to find something for her to wear. And when I did this last part, I had a breakdown inside the dress shop and ran out sobbing into my hands, snot running down my face, people staring at me, worried and freaked out. I hadn't been able to remember what size she was, or what type of bra to buy—does a dead woman even need a bra? I didn't know whether or not to buy shoes to go with the dress. No one would see her feet, she was dead! It turns out this bothered Cody's wife, Cara. I didn't buy Mom shoes to wear on her feet in a casket for the rest of her dead life, but I did buy her a simple wine-colored dress, a white scarf, and pearl earrings—and of course a bra and underwear. If they didn't get used, I didn't care. The process nearly killed me, and having Cara so upset that Mom wasn't wearing shoes made absolutely no sense to me.

Throughout the process, I had support. Lots of support. Jo basically held my hand through the whole process and guided me when I kept saying, "I don't know," and walking away, my muscles shaking, my head spinning, my world collapsing. Cara did Mom's hair and makeup, and she asked me with pleading eyes to help, and I refused.

"Do your best. Mom wouldn't mind what it looks like," I said to her, my back to them.

"Will you please just look?"

RAISED BY NARCOTICS —Floating

"No."

Shawn and his dad took over with Aryn. Ray was her favorite person in the world—still is—and he very easily stepped in to handle the four-year-old I hadn't talked to yet. Actually, I never did. I forgot to. Someone must have, but it wasn't me.

I stopped being a mother.

I stopped being a wife.

I wanted to stop being me.

I couldn't escape the life that had been handed to me, and somehow things just got worse and worse and worse.

At her funeral, I didn't know how to feel. I'm not a religious person, and I will tell you that hearing over, and over, and over again that my mother was in a better place, or that she was with my unborn child—all the things religious people say to show comfort and support—sent my mind careening off a cliff. It hurt so much more than it helped, and thus was born the girl who declared her atheism just to keep people around her grounded in reality so that they wouldn't accidentally offend her.

I stayed away from Mom's casket, only going close to it while I was tucked into Cody's arms and crying together. I couldn't do it alone. I wouldn't do it alone—not to mention how many people were showing up. How did Mom know this many people? Where the hell had they been all these months that we were struggling so bad and she was homeless?

Then, they walked in. The women from the shelter. Cody talked to them, reached out, hugged them, let them cry. He was so much better with people than I had ever been. He came over to me as I stood like a zombie watching the slideshow repeat itself, reliving my life over and over and over and over. He took my hand and took me to meet them. They stared at me, judging me, silently yelling at me for never coming to get her. I knew how much they loved her, and they said as much. In such a short time they had all bonded so well, like sisters. She had even been like a second mom to one of the smaller girls, a teenager. I saw the questions written on their faces: why wouldn't you come get your own mother and take care of her, when clearly you can afford a funeral like this? It was a beautiful funeral, but I didn't pay for it. Mom had paid for most of it over the years since Teresa died, and Jo took care of the flowers and the casket, but they didn't know that. I had everything, and my mother had nothing—and now I was grieving a woman I had refused to care for in her most desperate hour.

It dawns on me only now that Mom had never really cared about her life, but she cared very much about her death.

I said goodbye quickly and turned my back on them. I couldn't take it.

* * *

After the funeral, we stood outside in the snow, on a beautiful sunny day. I wore a white coat over the same black dress I had worn to two previous funerals, keeping my hands in my pockets and staring into the glare of the white, fluffy snow. It blinded me, but I did not look away.

RAISED BY NARCOTICS—Floating

A lot of people had gotten up and stood in front of her now-closed casket. I knew her body was in there, but I would never see it again. They spoke of her fondly, and I hated them all. I hated everyone who got up to speak any words about her, because it was all insincere, it was all fake and meaningless. Things people say out of obligation because the dead person is dead, and now everyone needs comfort, routine, and tradition. Ray read a poem about never having any more worries. Never feeling the cold again. Never needing anything again. It was a beautiful poem, one I wished I had written myself, but in that moment, I hated it and I hated him. How could he do that to me, and tear my heart open when it had only just broken? Yet, I had been the one to give him the go-ahead to read it. I needed him to say something because I had been too afraid that I wouldn't.

Aryn sat with her cousins, huddled under a blanket, giggling because they were together and that was how they were each happiest—together. They had each other, and it was truly the only thing that brought a smile to my face. It was the only sincere moment that had happened all day. That was a moment worth remembering because it was the only moment Mom would have appreciated.

I spoke some words too, but I never wrote anything down like I had at Teresa's. I didn't even know if I could do it, or if I would just stand there and look stricken—which I was and I did. Eventually though, the words came, and I was partly afraid of what I might say. Would I say the hard truths of everything we had been through? Would I yell at those who came today, but had never been there to support my mother before?

No.

I said nice things about her long hugs, and terrible goodbyes. I spoke about how she loved deeply and unconditionally, because it was true. Mom was a passionate person, at all times. The last thing I said, to cater to the audience and fill my heart with more hurt than I can ever remember feeling, was, "See you later, Mom."

That was it.

I stayed and handed little roses to the girls to play with while we watched everyone get into their cars and forget that Diane Nielsen had ever existed in this cruel and unforgiving world full of people just like them.

* * *

I went back to the funeral home and did the mundane little things like cleaning up now that the party was over—and things changed in me that I wasn't prepared for. Little things like taking home the flowers that had been set up to showcase Mom's beautiful life, thinking I could try to enjoy their beauty at home, until they started dying . . . I had to throw them out. I never wanted anything in my home again that would die like that. I couldn't even watch flowers die, and everyone sent me flowers. Even Meghan. I'm sorry Meghan. I set them up, took some photos to preserve their beauty and the gesture, but then threw them away before they had a chance to die inside of my home.

I had enough of death.

RAISED BY NARCOTICS—Floating

I tried hanging the canvas photos that I had printed of Mom in my house, but I couldn't look at her face anymore. I had to remove any trace of her. I put away everything that reminded me of her.

I couldn't look at her.

I couldn't think of her.

I couldn't stop thinking about her.

I didn't know how to feel.

When Teresa and Grandma Jane had died, I was sad. You're supposed to be sad. When Mom died, I felt everything. Guilt. Regret. Despair. Denial. Anger. Love. Sadness. Relief.

I wasn't grieving for just one person—now I was grieving for all three. And not just the three women I had lost, one every four years, but the life I had lost for myself. The life we had never lived. The normal life I had always wanted with these people that I loved. I would never know it now. They were all gone, all three of them, leaving me with this giant hole in the very center of my life. I didn't know how to navigate around it.

Were pregnancy hormones to blame for how I handled her death? They probably played a part, but it's also the thing that saved my life. I stood in the shower nearly every day, trying to maintain the warmth inside of my own body that I had lost. I couldn't tolerate cold anymore, and I needed escape. I would sit on the floor of the shower, letting the hot water hit me until it went cold, dreaming of running away to the sun, anywhere with the sun, but preferably the sun and the sand and the waves. The things that I loved, that made me feel whole. The things I wanted to lose myself in. I wanted to walk into the water and let it take me away.

But then there was a kick. A little flutter in my belly, one day while I sat in the shower. My little bundle reminding me that I wasn't alone.

CHAPTER 26
Control

After Mom died, I shut down emotionally. Pretty hard, actually. It got to such a bad point that I wasn't talking to anyone about anything that might make me feel—well, anything other than happiness. If I couldn't make them comfortable while they were around me, I was... I don't know. I don't know what I was, because I wasn't doing it for them. I wasn't even doing it for me. I simply existed and passively accepted the things that were happening around me.

Shawn and I were fighting all the time, and I ended up shutting him out of my emotional life altogether. I ended up shutting out Aryn, as well. Shawn had to take over parenting our daughter in nearly every aspect. I dropped her off and picked her up from school, I made sure she had things to do during her time away from school, but I wasn't parenting her in a meaningful way. I wasn't talking to anyone. Literally. I wasn't speaking—not intentionally, it just didn't occur to me to do so.

The only person I did talk to was Mandy, and that was because I would go to the salon where she worked—the one just down the street from my house, where I had been trying to get a job alongside her—because I was suffocating at home. I only went to her to complain. I never really opened up about my *real* pain, just the surface level stuff that came as a result of that pain. She never knew I wanted to take my own life, that the only thing stopping me was the little baby growing in my belly, and possibly the fact that she gave me sanctuary every Sunday by shampooing my hair and styling it for me.

We found out we were having a little boy in April 2012. I had decided if we were to have a girl, I would name her after my mother. Instead we had our little boy, Nicolas.

I'm so glad I didn't have a girl.

In the days leading up to his birth, I made a lot of decisions on how it was going to go. I made a birth plan, if you will. We all know that only about one in three birth plans go according to plan, but it didn't stop me from wanting full and complete control over everything—which is to say I wanted it to be very different from my experience with Aryn.

At six months pregnant, I discovered I had gestational diabetes. This was one of those lifesaving moments in my life. In little Nick's life. Shawn and I were fighting—or rather, I was fighting him internally and not really saying anything. He thought everything was fine. He was trying to better his life, and I hated him for every decision he was

RAISED BY NARCOTICS—Control

making because it threw away my plans for a normal and stable existence.

He decided to apply for graduate school. That's exciting, right? Well, he got rejected over and over and over again, to every single school he applied to. Nearly all our savings went into those applications, which wasn't much at the time—but when it's all you have to prepare for a new baby, it's too much. Not only that, but he quit his job, asked his parents to support us financially, and spent his days going to a part-time internship that might better his chances when it came time to apply again.

I was stuck in a situation so far out of my control that I wanted to end everything. My marriage, myself. I considered getting into my car with my two kids in tow and driving until I felt well and truly happy somewhere else. Who knew where that would have been?

I wanted out.

Badly.

But then, the diagnosis. My doctor told me that I needed to stay away from sugar and carbs. I didn't know what that meant. To me, that meant damn near everything. He set up an appointment for me to meet with a dietician who would explain everything, but it was two weeks out, and I was so paranoid about accidentally killing myself that I nearly stopped eating altogether. I find this statement almost funny, but it's true! I didn't know what to eat. I just knew I couldn't eat what I had been eating, and I don't think I would have cared nearly as much if it hadn't been for the health of the baby growing inside of me.

Once the appointment came, the dietician explained everything to me, and I faced a couple of decisions about my health. It gave me something to focus on, some piece of my life over which I could have some control. What I didn't have control of was how expensive it was. Being a diabetic is extremely expensive, especially when you suddenly have no insurance.

This is the beginning of a success story in my life that everyone just loves.

I weighed in at 207 pounds before getting pregnant.

One year after having Nicolas, I was at 157 pounds.

This success story is also one of complete darkness for me. It's the very thing I'm getting at with this entire book—well, not the weight loss itself, but . . . we'll get there.

My dietician set me up with new ways to think about food and my health. I poked my fingers six times a day to make sure I was doing it correctly and not about to go into a diabetic coma or have to go in for insulin injections. I took control because I had to. It was the only thing I could control.

The most important thing in my life was that I never became like them—Mom and Teresa. I never wanted to rely on medication for anything to get me through life, so I found a way around it. In this case it was the food I ate, and because of the restricted diet I was now on to keep me away from insulin shots, I started losing weight, even while I was pregnant. My doctor kept me reassured that it was safe and that the baby wouldn't suffer. The body has an incredible way of sorting out where everything needs to go. I started

RAISED BY NARCOTICS—Control

feeling better, both with the focus in my life, and the new way I was eating. My pregnancy became the best thing about me. I was in love with being pregnant—every single thing about it.

I think this gave my family a false perception of how I was really doing internally. I was so focused, so in love with the baby in my belly. I wasn't thinking about anything outside of the two of us. I was so enamored with it that everyone just assumed I was fine.

I found my control. I found a reason to survive. I found something to love, and I sat alone in my own world, feeling my belly, absorbed in who I was and what I would become to this little boy when he came home with me one day. I shut everything else out. There was no room for anyone else in my heart.

I still very much hated Shawn, but I knew I would work out what to do about it later. Right now, I needed me and this little boy to be healthy—and together. I would do anything to keep it that way.

When it came time to have my little boy, I had to be induced. There was no real way around it—I needed to have a healthy baby boy, and there was a specific time frame in which I wasn't risking his health as he came into this world. But I promised myself that I would avoid any other medication at all costs.

Unfortunately, it didn't go as planned. I ended up being pushed into having an epidural because I was at risk of delivering the placenta before my child. That might have killed him. I was so tense and stressed through the contractions that it almost happened, and my doctor made sure I had the epidural before it did. It was either that or have an emergency C-section. Both things out of my control.

So, what could I do? I had no choice, and I was mad, but my baby would soon be here and none of it would matter anyway.

I had watched medication kill my entire family, and I was so terrified of that happening to me that I pushed away any drugs offered to me. Even after my child was born, the nurses were flabbergasted—that's an accurate term—that I was refusing any pain medication. That didn't stop them from trying to get me to, and basically telling me I was crazy not to. There is a pressure to do so within hospital walls, and each new nurse who came in gave me the same runaround as the last. They all said I should be taking something, and they gave me the "Well, okay, it's your funeral" eye roll when I refused. Isn't that something?

At 11:55 p.m. on September 6, 2012, my son entered the world and instantly changed everything I thought I knew about love. I recall having complete tunnel vision for my boy, and my boy alone. The moment was perfect, and he was perfect. He had no complications, and he was a perfect eight pounds two ounces. They placed him on my chest for skin-to-skin, and my world stopped.

He was it.

He was everything.

Can I really explain this moment to someone who has never felt it? Has every mother felt this? I didn't feel it with

RAISED BY NARCOTICS—Control

my first-born. I loved her, but her birth was different. I was disconnected. This time, I was so absolutely connected to this little soul that I soon realized that it would nearly kill me to have him taken away from me.

It's not just that the moment was perfect. It's not just that he was perfect and healthy. It was simply that he was mine. I stopped loving everything else around me. How could I love anyone else? He needed me, and I needed him.

End of story.

That's not really the end, though, is it? And maybe I'm putting emphasis on the wrong thing entirely. It's important to me that you understand what happened to me emotionally, as well as why I made the decisions that I made.

Now, at twenty-six years old, I had lived through something that I didn't know how to handle. I had lived inside of a prescription medication drug ring, and then watched each person I thought I loved die. That was my normal, and now I was focused on creating a new normal.

After Mom passed away, I realized that my life *wasn't* normal. I realized that things needed to change, especially if I was going to be here for my little boy and raise him to be old enough to have some real memories of his mother before she took her own life. I had a few years yet to accomplish this. I wanted him to remember me, and I was still so unsure of my own life that I didn't know if I wanted to stick it out. For him though, I would. I would do anything for him, including giving him the life my husband wasn't willing to give us.

CHAPTER 27

A Different Life

Immediately after Nick's birth, Shawn and I started having horrendous fights. Now that we were a family of four, I was absolutely not okay living under his parents' thumb and having no independence of our own. Shawn had lost so much motivation. He blamed it on the new baby (who I almost never let him touch). He stopped going to his internship, so I started looking for a job on my phone while I rocked my sleeping boy in my arms. Shawn had ruined all my plans for a safe, secure, and stable home for me to bring my boy into. All I had wanted my entire pregnancy was to relax and enjoy the fleeting moments of being a new mom again. I craved those connections I never had with Aryn. Now I felt it was my responsibility to find a job and make that happen without him. I would be a new mom *and* a working mom, just to prove a point.

The truth about finding a job in a salon is that it's stupid easy. I had jobs lined up fast, because there is so much demand and turn-around within the industry. I knew it would happen, and I'm honestly glad to have such an in-demand career. Not one I could maintain a fancy lifestyle with, but one in which I could support myself and my two kids if I had to—and that's just what I did. I did *not* want to leave my son, though, so I decided to work part-time, while also using it to get under Shawn's skin. I took a job at a salon near our home only a month after Nick was born, and I continued yelling at Shawn as often as I could to get his shit together. Then I went behind his back to ask his mother to cut us off. She said she would give us until after the New Year, and I asked her to tell Shawn what she had just said to me. I wanted him to see that it was important to his parents that he become the person he needed to be for his family, because he just wasn't listening to me.

The fact that he wouldn't listen to them, or me, was another red flag in our relationship. I didn't trust him to do what he needed to do to take care of us, because we didn't share the same vision for what that was supposed to look like. Reluctantly he let go of his dreams of graduate school, and found a job, then another, and another. He had computer skills and hadn't been using them, for much the same reason I didn't want to use my styling skills, but now we both worked part time. In the end, he accepted a position working nights full-time for a company that provided some pretty great health benefits. It offered us the chance to be independent again. Shortly after that, I was finally accepted at the salon with Mandy, working a few days a week.

I can't say that I was happy, because Shawn and I just went right back to not speaking to each other. But I had the stable life I wanted again, and more control over our situation. And, of course, I loved getting the chance to work with Mandy on the weekends.

I worked every other morning, and thanks to the benefits of Shawn's new job, I was actually set up with a virtual health coach to continue losing weight and gaining perspective on my health after the gestational diabetes. I was incentivized by the fact that if I met certain goals each month, his company would match the money we put into our health savings account. We were set, and I was incredibly motivated to change my health and goals in life. As soon I was cleared to start exercising, I set up my treadmill that had been collecting dust and took my first run. I chose running for a few reasons. The first was watching some of my Facebook friends do it. They were running races and making it look fun. The second was an almost natural impulse to do so, as if I might be literally running away from my problems. I loved walking (I could walk for hours on end!), but I had very little experience with running—and let's not forget trying to get into the Army. Even so, running just seemed like the easiest thing I could pick up, and it helped a lot that the sport was trending all over social media. I didn't need to be good at it, I just needed to try. Put one foot in front of the other, as they say, and use the physical pain of building endurance to kill the emotional pain I was feeling every day.

That was December 2012.

RAISED BY NARCOTICS—A Different Life

Almost one year after Mom had passed, my life was completely different. I was working. I had my son who was with me every moment that I wasn't at work. I was focused on my health and making significant changes in my lifestyle. My marriage was silently falling apart. I never saw Shawn anymore, and I honestly didn't want to. I preferred it that way. We never saw eye-to-eye, and I was working on how I could leave and be a single mother. I was feeling stronger every single day, and the more I ran, the better I felt about my decisions to take control of my life. I hated life still, but I needed the one thing I had never had before—independence.

I worked, I ran, and I took care of my kids. I pushed away my husband, but with my daughter I took a different approach. I hated my emotions, so I suppressed them. She got what probably seemed like an okay mommy, but I was more like a zombie toward her than a mother. I let her do whatever she wanted, with minimal expectations. She was alive, and happy; she had friends, and things she enjoyed doing. She loved being a second mommy to her little brother, and I let her be involved. I didn't yell, I didn't praise—I just was. It's as if all my emotion had been reserved for my little boy, and it's probably very obvious to her what happened. For that, my little Aryn, I'm so sorry. All I can say is: that's how I coped. I didn't know what I was doing. I could only do what felt right, and that was it. I hadn't been given any instructions on how to be a good mother. I knew how not to be a *bad* mother, but I didn't know how to be a good one. Not in the way that it mattered most.

Still to this day, I am disconnected—to not just her, and not just Shawn, but to everyone who isn't Nick.

What was really happening was that I was floating on the high I had created for myself in losing so much weight and getting so much praise and attention from my friends online via Facebook and Instagram.

"You're so amazing, Alyse!"

"Way to go girl, you're smokin'!"

"I'm so inspired by your dedication, you have to tell me what you're doing!"

I posted picture after picture of my progress, even one where I'm wearing an old pair of size 18 jeans and holding out the sides, so people could really see just how much I had lost. Fifty pounds, man, that's nothing to sneeze at. I was damn proud of who I was becoming—and not just that, but my running had really taken off. I was doing 5k's, 10k's, and I was getting ready for my very first half marathon. Everyone was so impressed, inspired, and—dare I say—jealous. I loved that they envied me. I needed that feeling so desperately in my life. The positive affirmation, the attention . . . I craved it.

As I floated on my high of being a new person, I was hiding behind a mask of pain. I knew it was there. I started realizing what was happening, but I still couldn't fully face it. I think Shawn tried talking to me, but every time he did, I literally ran away. I stood up, walked away from him, and focused on something else. I thought he was being rude and

RAISED BY NARCOTICS—A Different Life

annoying. We were getting along in a passive way, but I hid everything from him and from myself as much as I could. I lived in denial. I still refused to look at pictures of Mom, and if anything reminded me of her, I very quickly distracted myself.

Mom was gone, nothing to be done, move the fuck on, Alyse.

I kept myself busy, not happy. We had a good life, but I hated it. I hated everyone around me, and everything going on.

I resented everyone. One of Shawn's sisters had come to me one day not long after Nick was born, telling me that she was so inspired by my love for my little boy, and my strength as a mother, that she decided to have kids of her own. I was touched when she told me, but completely pissed after she had her baby and broke down into postpartum depression. It was so severe that she coasted on medication to get through her days, never touching her baby and making either her mother, Jo, or her mother-in-law, sit with her, literally day and night, to take care of her and her child.

I have struggled in my life, but never with postpartum depression. To say I understand it would be a great disservice to anyone who has ever experienced it. What I experienced was something else entirely, and I hated what she went through, and what Jo did for her when she went through it. Who had been there for me when I had just lost my mother and had my son, and pushed away my husband and daughter? When I was suicidal every day of my life, and had no one to talk to about it? No one came to check on me, none of my neighbors came by with dinners to help in my time of need. No, I did everything on my own. I fixed my own life, on my own, with no help, and fuck everyone around me for never being there.

It felt like that was thrown in my face every day that I saw Jo's car pull into their garage—and stay all day. We all lived much too close together, and every day that I saw it, I wanted to die. I was worthless. It didn't matter how strong I was being on the outside, how inspiring that strength was to everyone around me. I wanted to end my worthless life, a life that no one had ever cared about, and never would.

It was so clear to me that I didn't matter. I started having days where I would lock myself alone in my room and stare at the gun-safe on Shawn's side of the bed, wondering if I really did remember the code to get to the gun sleeping inside. Then I'd force myself to forget it, because I knew what I would finally do if I was able to open it. I would pull the trigger.

I can't tell you what stopped me time and time again. I think I really did believe that I had forgotten the code, and it ultimately stopped me from trying. Besides, my son wasn't yet old enough to remember me if I left this world, so I stayed for him.

In October 2013, Shawn was interviewed by a start-up company close to our home for a position that would pay much more than he was making now—more than we were making together, in fact. I could quit and finally stay home with my baby, the very thing I had wanted since he was born. But it wasn't out of state, something I had been

RAISED BY NARCOTICS—A Different Life

hoping for since I was a teenager desperate to get out of a bad situation, and a state full of people that didn't understand me. I always felt like the black sheep, the girl who never fit in anywhere. Living through any more Utah winters felt unbearable, but this opportunity was still in Utah. Oh well, we were settled here. I wasn't going to say no to that. I wasn't going to love it, but I wasn't going to say no. Everything just worked here, so whatever.

Every October we have a tradition to invite our friends over to watch a scary Halloween movie. We call it Halloween Movie Night. I'm creative like that. Halloween is by far my favorite holiday, and with my history with Shawn and Jo's infamous Halloween parties, well, it just made sense. Halloween was also the night when I first met everyone in Shawn's family, including Meghan, Cory, and their girls. It's not just a movie night—it's really a celebration of the anniversary when these people came into my life. I don't have any other traditions like this for any other time of year, but I love this one night when I can dress up, put on an actual mask, invite my closest friends over, and laugh over scary movies. The point is, it's fun. And it's a chance for me to show off my culinary skills that I have developed over the years, especially preceding my healthy lifestyle. It serves as a reminder that I do in fact have people in my life, despite how stubborn I am to show my real face.

In the middle of this traditional get together, Shawn got the call he had been waiting for with the official offer for the exciting new job. I knew what it was and I was so excited for him, and for us. This would be a huge step up for our lifestyle. Shawn came in with his hand over the phone, as if someone was still on the phone, and he looked at me concerned. I was really confused.

"They want to talk to you," he whispered.

"What? Why?"

"I don't know."

"okay," I said, apprehensively taking his phone, my nerves kicking into high gear instantly. It was like the anxiety slapped me in the face. I still couldn't face stress of any kind, even a simple phone call.

I took the phone into the back room to talk to what would hopefully be Shawn's new boss.

He admitted immediately that this was weird. *No kidding*, I thought. But he wanted my opinion on Shawn since he was considering him for the job—like a reference. He explained that they were very family-oriented, and of course he wanted Shawn's wife's endorsement. Well, he was certainly going to get it, because this wasn't just Shawn's life on the line, it was mine. I didn't know what to say about my own husband, though. I was completely speechless. I was stuck interviewing for a job that wasn't going to be mine, and I didn't know what I could say for a man I didn't love or even really like all that much. I think he took it to be that he had caught me off guard, and gave me some examples of what Shawn's other reference had already said. I just nodded my head and said, "Yeah, ummm, I mean he's a really a great guy. He's really funny, he's very family-centric and dedicated," mimicking what had already been said about him.

RAISED BY NARCOTICS—A Different Life

I felt like I couldn't endorse my husband, but I needed him to have this job. If they had known what I was really thinking...

"He's a selfish bastard who has neglected me and everything I've gone through. I think I want a divorce. In fact, I know that I do, but I'm too afraid to say it to him, because I don't know how I would make being a single mother work out yet, despite living in an already rich family. I don't know how much I'm entitled to. I need him to have this job, so that I can take half of his money when he gets a promotion, and I can safely save enough to leave him at random when I've finally had enough."

Until that phone call, I hadn't really understood how I felt. He got the job that night, and we celebrated with our friends and family, and I hid even more behind the mask I had created for myself. I watched my husband celebrate his success surrounded by people in his life who had always loved him, supported him, and given him a reason to want to live.

How could I not be excited for him and the money it would mean for our family? The new opportunities? Maybe I would finally get my shit together, find myself, or give myself a damn break. I don't know, it just meant good things.

I struggled constantly with the feeling of "I can get through this, things can be different," and "Oh my god I can't stand it anymore I need out!" I truly felt like I was going crazy. I knew I needed something, but I just didn't know what it was, how to get it, or who to talk to.

Throughout the next year, we enjoyed where we were. Shawn and I celebrated our eighth anniversary by meeting our friends, Meghan and Cory, in Disneyland. For the first time in two years, I started seeing this man with different eyes. We actually had a lot of fun together when it was just us and no kids. I almost didn't want to go home, but my baby needed me—and more importantly, I needed him. Of course, right before we left, both kids got an ear infection—curses for having a winter anniversary! Still, the grandparents were very willing to stay home with them and take care of them. They all did just fine, and Shawn and I started reconnecting and I started reevaluating my life . . . again.

The year was a bit of a blur, and not all that interesting, but it's important to note that I started coming out of my shell a little more with Shawn, which inevitably meant more fights because my back was always up against a wall. I blame a lot of those fights on me. I didn't want to see his perspective; I just desperately wanted him to see mine. What those fights meant, though, was that at least I was communicating. Little by little I realized I couldn't just let my shutdown continue forever. I needed out of my own head, but even so, I was still a very quiet person. I have always been called the "cute, quiet girl." While I was growing up, it was somehow a thing to call me cute or quiet. Have you ever wondered why people are quiet? It's not cute at all. I feel that the quiet ones, potentially, have the most to say, and there's probably a huge reason why they're quiet.

Even in my own home I was the shy, quiet girl. I was also the quiet mom, so when it became apparent that my

RAISED BY NARCOTICS—A Different Life

son wasn't meeting normal toddler milestones, I started blaming myself. I wasn't the type of mom to narrate my child's life, or talk while we played with toys, or sing him to sleep. We weren't to a point where story time was routine. When we played, I just sat and watched him, let him hand me toys, or passed toys back to him, or just showed him what to do with a toy. We didn't have a communicative relationship—we just sat together playing. He watched me in the kitchen sometimes, playing at his own little kitchen, trying to make noises. The only noise he really liked saying was "gum" or "agum." He would ramble "agum, agum, agum" for everything. Everything was "agum."

In the summer of 2014, as he neared two years old, I started getting really worried. I took him to his eighteen-month checkup with his normal doctor—the same one who had delivered him, the only doctor I trusted—and he said, "Try not to worry, at this age everyone goes at their own pace." Telling me to try not to worry was laughable, though. I hadn't even trusted my own doctor enough to tell him how horribly depressed and suicidal I was because I was afraid he would put me on antidepressants, and I absolutely refused. I ran, I ate healthy. He encouraged my healthy lifestyle, and I said I was fine, so I left it at that. What more could I do for myself than be a healthy person? If you're healthy, you don't need that shit.

So, of course, I nearly worried to death. I called Jo to see if she would have lunch with me to talk about it. I couldn't open up about myself, but I could get some motherly advice in this area from the only other mother in my life who had successfully raised six children, one of whom is a very high-functioning autistic adult. That's immediately where she went with it. She told me—with no doubt in her mind—that Nick had autism. He had all the signs, and her boy was the exact same way. I wanted to run screaming from the cafe. It had been a mistake to pick my favorite one where people knew me by name, because otherwise I would have done just that.

Now, don't get me wrong. Having a child with a disability can be a struggle, but it also doesn't have to be the end of the world. When it's your own child, you know you'll go to the ends of the earth to help them through life, no matter what their struggle. That is exactly what I was prepared to do, but I hadn't been prepared to face that type of problem—besides, Jo is no doctor, and my doctor had given no indication of being concerned about autism (although he did only spend roughly ten minutes with us; hardly enough time to get to know my little boy at our appointments every few months).

I was scared. Mental illness of any kind was terrifying to me, and I was pretty sure I, myself, was crazy in some fashion and in complete denial. I couldn't possibly face it in my own child. Could I? I didn't know who to talk to.

One afternoon while hoping to talk to anyone—not necessarily about this, but just as a friend—I called up a neighbor to get our boys together to play at the splash pad. She was very much a hermit like I was, but lo and behold, she had all the answers I needed! Right after that, she texted me the resources that she had used for her own boy who

RAISED BY NARCOTICS—A Different Life

had struggled in a similar fashion. That, I'll tell you, was just lucky. Although I claim to be an atheist, it's moments like this that make me question everything I think I stubbornly know about the universe.

When I got home from our play date, I called the number she had given me. I had some anxiety about what they would say, but what could it hurt? The foundation was called Kids On The Move, or KOTM. They focused on all kinds of delays in children, including those with Down syndrome and those who fall on the autism spectrum. They immediately set me up with an appointment for someone to come to my home to test Nick in things like gross motor skills, vision, hearing, and speech. They were very thorough and made it all about him. It was fascinating to watch, and when he did something well, my heart swelled with pride.

In the end, they sat going over all the papers with me, and they told me straight away that he wasn't on the autism spectrum. He was close to it, but not on it, so the first thing to do was to get him his own speech therapist who would come work with him twice a week. The very best part was the cost, or lack thereof. Because it was a non-profit, it was all income-based, and we ended up paying something like $20 a month for his visits.

What I say next is one of those moments in life. Those turning points I talk about. My son having a speech delay, and a little bit of a physical one as well, was as much a blessing in my life as gestational diabetes had been. It changed everything—not because of his delay, but because of who it brought into our lives.

Her name was Alex, and she was so bubbly and sweet from the get-go that it was unnerving. When she arrived, she did what the other two women had done: she brought out her big bag of toys, sat with Nick, and played. She showed me how to help him start making sounds, and how to praise him as he went along. We sat like that for nearly an hour, and I learned so much, but I was also scared of it all. I really was quiet, too quiet, when I interacted with my son. He started picking things up so quickly, and I couldn't help but realize that it was probably my fault for never really communicating with him. She told me I needed to narrate everything we did, that it would sound funny and I would laugh at myself, but it would be something he could mimic and learn from. She was right—it was really strange for me. My muscles felt like they were spasming as I tried to do the same things she was doing with my own son while she sat there guiding us, and near the end I could hardly breathe anymore. I started developing a really terrible headache.

What she did next was what really changed the direction of my life. She was wrapping up our session, and we sat down on the couch going over the papers, when she asked me, "How are you doing?" She said it so passively, my first response was, "What?"

For some reason I really couldn't wrap my head around what she was asking.

"I'm really sorry, I don't know what you mean," I replied, nervously.

The look on her face said everything, and I think it's because of how I reacted to her question. I mean, people

RAISED BY NARCOTICS—A Different Life

didn't just ask me how I was doing—ever, not even casually. How was I doing? God, if I could only tell her!

"I mean it, how are you doing? This type of thing can be overwhelming, and we're here not just for your child, but for you as the parent, as well. For your whole family, really."

I couldn't handle it. She was just so sincere. I had never met anyone like her in my entire life, and I had known her for less than an hour. I was sitting sideways on the couch, one leg resting underneath me, completely casual as I faced her for our conversation. But as soon as she asked her question, I brought my hands to my face and started sobbing. I was so not okay, and here was the first person to ask me that question since my mother died.

I didn't know how much time she had, and she looked really baffled at my tears, so I said what I could as fast I could through my snot as I sobbed. She actually had tissues on hand. Where did those even come from? Her purse?

"I think my marriage is falling apart, and my mom died, and my son can't talk, and I don't know how I'm doing, I can't handle my life."

Shit, even now I'm crying just writing that.

That moment was so powerful. I really wasn't okay, and for the first time someone was listening, and even looked like she cared. From that moment forward she made it her job to help me find the help I needed, even if that was just talking to her for the first little while. During our first few appointments, she would set an extra hour aside after working with Nick to talk to me.

Alex is such a crucial piece of where I'm at today—each moment in life, becoming a piece of such a large and complicated puzzle. Maybe you've started to connect the dots. When you're on the outside looking in, a lot seems more obvious, but it would take me a few years from this time with Alex to piece things together. I was still in denial, because it's easier to deny the truth—especially when you can't go back in time to fix any of it.

CHAPTER 28

Changing Perspective

Alex helped me in so many ways through KOTM. They offered several parenting classes, and a daycare so that Shawn and I could attend together. He and I started working with Nick together and involving Aryn in the process. She was so excited to help her little brother learn how to talk, and she really fell into that role with everything she had. Every moment of our lives became more animated, and I learned to use my voice again. It was so important for me to listen to Alex's advice on how to help Nick, so I stupidly went around the house with him talking about everything that we were doing. But in a very short time, it just became what we did. His milestones with his speech completely validated the entire process, but it also confirmed my guilt.

The second most important thing Alex did for me was connect me with a support group. I was very leery of this idea, especially considering that it was really for moms struggling with children with much larger disabilities than

Nick's. But she invited me to come, and I did. Nick was able to play with some kids his age in the daycare for an hour every week, and I was able to sit in a room full of women who didn't judge me or look down on me for struggling the way that I did, even if it was different than how they did. What I learned there was how to communicate, how to cope. I didn't open up very often, but I learned again how to be a normal friend. Someone who talks to people. I had been suppressing everything I was going through—even healthy things, and shutting everyone out in doing so. Running had become what cutting used to be for me in my teen years, a way to release the horrible emotion. It was easier to feel a physical pain I could tolerate better than the deep, unrelenting sadness in my heart. I decided running was good for me. It was my antidepressant, because I liked how it made me feel—and of course it was much more productive than using a razor blade to draw blood.

Even as an adult, I had done things like get too many piercings and a couple of tattoos. I loved, and still crave, the raw feeling of a fresh tattoo. I might be covered in them if not for being afraid of it ruining any career opportunities I might have in the future. The point is, I use physical discomfort to release my emotion, and there can be productive ways of doing so without hurting myself. I started doing yoga as well, and really getting into it. Not so much these days, but I would like to do it again.

Throughout our time with Alex, she helped my son meet his milestones and eventually test out of speech therapy just after his third birthday. 2016 was quickly

RAISED BY NARCOTICS—Changing Perspective

approaching, and Shawn and I had been saving for our big ten-year anniversary. We wanted to go back to Maui, to where it all started, and revisit the passion we once had for each other.

Life was treating us well. He had kept his job at the start-up company, which was growing pretty damn fast, and each year they shared a new benefit. Then Shawn got promoted. Each year life was a little better, and I felt a little stronger, emotionally speaking.

In November 2015, I thought I might try my hand at National Novel Writing Month, affectionately shortened to NaNoWriMo. The idea is that you write 50,000 words in one month. My writer buddies will know what I'm talking about. It may not have originally been intended for memoir writing, but it was one of my first attempts at writing a story that went along with my own. I had already been piecing together my story, using my writing as an outlet to relive what I had gone through and figure out the puzzle of my life. It's not an easy thing to do, to reflect on all of that negativity and try to remain sane afterward. Maybe it's the very thing that's kept me depressed all these years, but I felt it so deep inside of my bones—I knew that I needed to do this. I needed to not stop until it was done. It wouldn't be perfect, and every writer has to accept that. I mean, look at the life I've lived—I'm taking such a massive mistake of a life and handing it to you to pick apart. Take what you need to hear and use it to reevaluate what you're going through. Talk to just one person.

*   *   *

When 2016 started, Shawn and I were about to celebrate ten years of marriage. I knew things needed to change. I knew we needed to talk it all through. We'd been slowly reconnecting, and ever so slowly he was becoming the very thing I needed but had refused to be all those years—my soulmate, my best friend—no, more than that. We're not there yet though.

Just before our big trip to Hawai'i, I was very upfront with him. This was it for me. Part of me didn't even want to go to Hawai'i with him. I still held on to such deep resentment. It had been a complete stranger who had gotten me the help I needed, and encouraged me to really start focusing on my emotions—but not the man I had married. My husband was supposed to be the person who supported me through thick and thin, and he just wasn't.

I told him—very honestly, very calmly, with tears in my eyes—that I didn't know if I would stay or not after we came home from Hawai'i. I told him divorce was very real in my head. He absolutely didn't want that, but he understood where I was coming from. He was patient and let me explain myself, and somehow, we connected over it. He listened, in a very compassionate way. How strange? This had really never happened before.

The point, though, isn't our marriage. It's about family. The entire book is about family, and what that word means.

Family.

RAISED BY NARCOTICS—Changing Perspective

So many people have, what they feel, is a very obvious understanding of that word—but not me. Not until very recently, at least.

By the time Maui rolled around, I had used my pain and grief—the inner turmoil that I lived with daily—to run the fat right off my body. I was proud of myself. I was making a difference in my life, a profound change to never ever be anything close to what my mother or Teresa were—or hell, even Grandma Jane. Getting pregnant with Aryn had finally gotten me to give up smoking. Getting pregnant with Nick had refocused my brain on my health and caused a dramatic shift in the way I saw and thought of food.

Through my grief I started writing, thousands upon thousands of words, trying to piece together who I was, and why it all happened, and find a way to share it with the world in such a way as to make a meaningful impact on it. In that writing, I realized so many things, and through that—coupled with the help of Nick's speech therapy group, my new friends, my old friends, and my sweet little family—I started opening up a little more. I focused on my relationships and what each relationship in my life meant. I had changed in so many ways, and all for the better. After an entire lifetime of struggle, lack of support, and tons of heartaches and miscommunications, I was finally becoming a normal person, living inside of a normal family, with normal hopes, dreams, and traditions.

I had witnessed my own mother push every single person who loved her out of her life. Belittle them, use them, manipulate them, yell at them. She was a victim, and she made sure the world knew it. But because of it, she was incredibly lonely, which of course, only made matters worse for her and for those of us trying to be around her, because nothing we ever did—nothing *I* ever did—was ever good enough for her. She would always need more. She would never accept the people around her for who they were, or what they had to give. And because of that, she isolated herself. I didn't want to become that.

Everything my mother had been, I never wanted to be.

So, I tried—hard—to change who I was. I grew up with that woman, and I was like her in so many ways. From my hair, to my skin, to my mannerisms—as I grew older, even my voice sounded like hers, especially the way I yelled at my children. In my own grief, I developed resentment. It makes sense why I would feel that way, but it's not productive. I would end up just like her, leaving the only man who had ever accepted me, flaws and all, because he hadn't known what I needed when I fell apart. I didn't know what I needed when I fell apart, either—so that's hardly fair to him.

I can't remember where I read this or heard this, or if someone said it to me, but it boils down to this: the people offering support to those who are struggling need their own support.

Shawn couldn't support me, because he didn't have the support he needed to know how to support me. I couldn't support my mother, who couldn't support her sister, who was being supported by my grandmother, who didn't have the support to hold her emotions together. She shut down

RAISED BY NARCOTICS—Changing Perspective

much the same way I did, but she was never able to face it. Instead, she died.

Support is so crucial. Think of the sayings: "When momma ain't happy, ain't nobody happy," or "Happy wife, happy life" (which I hate), or this one "Depression affects everyone around you." That last one isn't really a saying, but a profound statement used in anti-depression medication ads around the globe to cause guilt and sell drugs—and yet it is no less true than the others.

My point is, we use medication as a support when we think those around us can't or shouldn't be bothered by us, or when those of us who are the supporters don't know how to support.

As we sat on the plane, headed for Maui, I pulled out my very first journal in years. It was a New Year's resolution of mine to put myself back together and find better ways to process my emotions so that I could save my marriage, and myself. I vowed to myself in that journal that I would write this book. I made that promise to myself on that long flight to paradise. I was stepping into the new life I never knew I wanted; the life I completely took for granted, yet lived in every single day.

I made a vow to look deep into the meanings of what it was to be married to the man sitting next to me, hoping for the same things to save us—maybe even make a new us. I reflected on the fact that when I came home, I would be staring in the face of another four years passing since one of my family members died and wondering—actually trying not to become hysterical with anxiety—if I would lose someone else. The what ifs played in my mind: what if this was it? What if it was my turn now, and I died on this plane, flying across the ocean to the good life I never should have had? What if Shawn died before we had a chance to really be in love and live a happy normal life together and do the things we said we would someday? Like sailing on our own boat from island to island? What if one of my children died, in whatever awful way children die?

I've known without a shadow of a doubt that if I were ever to lose my son, I would also kill myself. I will. Even after I write this book, even when I'm old, if I lose him, I will end my life—but in this year, the fourth year, what if it was my daughter? I couldn't end my life because I had my son who still needed me. Aryn had her daddy, and they would have to face their struggles together, but Nick was mine. I took full ownership, in a very codependent kind of way. But if Aryn were the one to die? And I had to live with that? Could I?

What if it was Cody this time? He was always exhausted from working too hard and struggling in his own life in his own ways. Also, doing dangerous things—he would probably die from something stupid like the Crocodile Hunter did (don't get me wrong, I loved Steve Irwin growing up. I might have even had a bit of a crush, but isn't it ironic? Don't you think? All the crazy things he was known for, and what actually happened completely blindsided everyone, including him? It's almost a joke, even though it's not a funny one.) That is just Cody's personality. He and I have already talked about it: with him, I wouldn't

RAISED BY NARCOTICS—Changing Perspective

be allowed to be sad if he did, because he was the only person I knew who truly lived an authentic life. He never held himself back from the things he wanted to do or try. If he accidentally killed himself pursuing something he loved, well, then, dammit Cody!

Four years is a long time, and either things came in threes, or I was about to lose someone else in 2016. Getting through that year would be very hard.

I am the kind of person who lives in fear, and that fear comes from a very real place—but isn't grounded in reality, if that makes any sense. Like telling Shawn to text me that he made it to work every single morning, or I would slowly lose my mind imagining the fiery car crash he was involved in, expecting the cops to come to my door any minute. I live like this. I still ask him to do it. I say it every day, and every day he texts me, "Made it to work, I love you." I do this to my daughter now that she rides her bike to school.

"Do you have your phone?"

"Yes Mom."

"Text me when you get to school."

That's all she uses her phone for, and I have a long string of messages that all say the same thing: "At school now." She doesn't understand why I make her do it. I'm just a helicopter Mom who wants to make sure she isn't getting kidnapped on the short ride to school.

So, is my family really cursed?

CHAPTER 29

The Last Straw

When Nick was 5 months old, he was hospitalized for RSV, respiratory syncytial virus. He and I spent the night at the hospital while he got the boogers jamming up his airways sucked out with a long thin tube, screaming the entire time. He was put on oxygen and was given breathing treatments from a little machine called a nebulizer. Ultimately, in an effort to both be home in our comfort zone and reduce the bills that inevitably came with hospital stays, we ended up buying a nebulizer to bring home. We even rented an oxygen tank after the nurses sat with us explaining how and when to use it at home. After five days like that at home, we were able to get the clear that he was on the mend. We continued doing a few breathing treatments at home morning and night, and the oxygen tank was picked up and sent back. RSV was a term I had heard before. A scary term, but something I knew could affect my little guy who was born just before winter had set in. Turns out most kids get it in their first winter, and not only once, but several times in their first years of life. My son was not an exception.

Every year we dealt with the colds that I had assumed Aryn was bringing home from school. He would get sick several times, have a hard time breathing through the snot in his face, and I would go to bed every night not being able to sleep for fear of watching one of my children die.

I became really frustrated with doctor visit after doctor visit, bill after bill. It was starting to feel like there was something more wrong with our son. During the summer months Nick would cough and cough and cough. I thought he was just getting more colds, but only he was getting sick, never the rest of us. We would have to stop what we were doing, whether at the park or a relative's home, sit Nick down and calm him down with a glass of water. Upon a suggestion from Nick's Uncle Matt, Shawn's little brother, we took him back in to see our doctor yet again. This time Nick didn't test positive for any virus or infection, and our doctor finally came back to us with the term "restrictive airways." He handed us a little inhaler and showed us how to use it for when he started coughing like that. I asked, "Is this asthma?"

To which the doctor replied, "We call it restrictive airways with kids his age, because most grow out of it by the time they're five or six."

Was that an answer to my question?

I nodded. We had this new inhaler, we had the nebulizer at home with a prescription for more albuterol to pour into it for when these episodes happened, and yet, I didn't really know what I was doing. I thought I did, and I believed that our doctor was working with us to give us the right answers, but I quickly found out that so much more could have been done to prevent what happened next.

It was October of 2016 and Nick had just started his first official year of preschool, so of course he was bound to bring home some type of germ to infect the family, and lo and behold, he did. He began with what seemed like a normal cold, but he was still my active little boy who just had a runny nose. I decided that despite the runny nose, we would take a bike ride. I was hard pressed to give up the beautiful day outside. I wanted to go find solace in the outdoors, like we always did, before winter officially hit and who knew how depressed I would become.

He started coughing a bit, like he always did, and we came home early. I had made plans to take Aryn out that night and spend some mother-daughter time with her to show her that I did in fact still care about her, even though I knew I was being distant and spending most of my time with her little brother. So, the two of us went out with instructions for daddy to keep our baby boy resting and relaxing.

When I came home, everything went downhill fast. It was nearing bedtime, and upon arriving home, I found my son standing on the couch. Then sitting, standing, sitting. He was restless. He couldn't keep himself still, and when I walked up closer to him, I could hear him struggling to breathe. Before now it had always just been a cough. Now, he really couldn't get any air, and he was agitated. I could tell he didn't know how to express that. He was breathing so hard I didn't know what to do. I grabbed the medicine from the counter—the all-natural stuff—to help him sleep through it. Massive mistake. He did fall asleep. I picked him up off the couch and carried him to his bed, feeling his little chest rising and falling rapidly, and there I stood watching him, not daring to leave his side. He lay in his bed, his little eyes closed, as if he were sleeping, but his chest still rose and fell as if it were crushing his little body, and it just wouldn't let up. I couldn't stand watching it, so I grabbed him, put on my shoes and jacket, and loaded him into the car to go to the clinic, yet again.

Something had to be done, even if it was just to have a doctor monitoring him instead of a scared mother who didn't know what she was doing.

I left Shawn home to stay with Aryn and get her into bed. He was as wide-eyed and scared as I was, thinking that he had done everything wrong. I had given him grief by yelling: "I can't leave the house for even an hour without shit hitting the fan!" and "When are you going to make decisions to take care of your own child instead of just playing video games while he's clearly agitated? Give him a bath, a breathing treatment, call me for Christ's sake!"

I stormed out of our home carrying my little boy who could hardly breathe. He woke up enough to be carried into the clinic and held onto me tightly. I told him how brave he was being, and I was sorry for waking him up, but mommy was so worried.

Usually when we arrived at the clinic to check in, we had to wait around in the waiting room until our name was called. But when we arrived and I said, "My son is having a hard time breathing," they sent us straight back, no time at all to sit down. The doctor, not ours but a woman I had never seen before, came into our room, lifted up his shirt, and saw for herself what was happening. She ordered some albuterol and a mask to help him breathe in the medicine and calm down his little chest. All the while I just sat watching, dumbfounded, when she suddenly said, "I think we'll go ahead and call the ambulance instead of having you drive to the ER." As if we had just been discussing it, which we had not.

"I'm sorry, the ambulance? Is it that bad?" I had no idea. I suddenly felt the weight of her words hit me. Another ambulance coming for another of my family members, because who knew if he would survive me taking him to the ER on my own.

What was happening?

He was awake and he was breathing, but not well enough. She started explaining to me—as I began to hear the distant blare of the sirens getting closer—that with what he was going through, he needed lifesaving equipment on hand in case he stopped breathing on his own. She said it could happen very quickly, and she didn't want to take any chances. Well, of course I agreed, but I was now in shock at what was happening.

The crew rushed into our room, and Nick was sitting in my lap facing them, a mask over his mouth to keep him

RAISED BY NARCOTICS—The Last Straw

breathing in the medication to open his airways. He was put onto a bed and carried into the ambulance, where I sat by his side, trying my hardest not to have a complete meltdown.

I was saved from it by his awesome little personality. He kept telling me that it was the most amazing thing to get to ride in a fire truck! He didn't know the difference between the two, and I didn't care. I just laughed with him, and squeezed his little fingers in my hand.

This was one of the longest nights of my life, because I knew that if I had let him try to sleep it off in his own bed, which I had almost done, I would have woken up to a dead child, and life as I knew it would be over. I could not cope with that knowledge. It scared the hell out of me.

I didn't call Shawn to tell him what had happened or where we eventually ended up until we were there, and Nick was resting as comfortable as possible in a bed, holding on tightly to a little race car the ambulance technician had given to him.

When I heard Shawn's voice, I didn't know if I wanted him sitting here with me, but it hardly mattered—Nick wasn't my child, he was *ours*, and if Shawn wanted to be here, he should be here. I asked him to bring me a few things on his way up, and while I waited for him to arrive, I sat in the chair next to Nick's bed, finally letting the severity of what had happened sink in. I told myself to breathe, I told myself to stay strong. I told myself that I would do whatever it was I had to do to stay with Nick and make sure he got what he needed. I resolved to yell at any and all doctors that crossed our path until I was given some serious answers about what he was dealing with.

Nick spent all night being monitored, and I was happy to be in a hospital with trained people taking care of my son, rather than home trying to make it up. The next day, he was already doing much better. They had saved his life—not only that, but I was now being sat down with more papers, and a doctor telling me he most definitely had asthma. Good, I didn't have to yell at anyone.

I played through the previous day as I sat with this new, yet obvious, information and tried to think through the cause for his asthma attack.

Our bike ride.

I would later find out that he has severe allergies to basically everything that grows outside, especially during certain seasons, and our little bike ride that day had set off a reaction that would later result in the near-death of my son. I started getting angry all over again at everyone, including myself.

This could have been prevented if I had been given the support and tools I needed to help my son overcome a diagnosis my doctor refused to give out prematurely. What did it take to diagnose a child who couldn't breathe? His near-death experience? *You asshole!*

This was truly my last straw with the medical industry, and not only that, but how badly it set us back financially. That one night cost us over $4,000, for what amounted to a really awesome car ride, breathing treatments, and being hooked to oxygen in a hospital. The same thing I could have

RAISED BY NARCOTICS—The Last Straw

done at home had I been taught and prepared. If I'd known how to handle the situation, I feel like we could have prevented the entire trip to the ER.

The irony was now we had hit our deductible, and I was going to use that to finally find the treatment and care my son deserved to understand what he was going through and learn how we could help him. Not just in the short term, but in the long term. I will be, along with my husband and my daughter, the support my son needs to overcome his obstacles, and I will never hesitate again to ask what needs to be asked or say what needs to be said.

I will not lose another family member to a completely preventable circumstance. Never again.

In the year of 2016, four years after Mom had passed, I couldn't believe that it had nearly happened again.

CHAPTER 30

I Didn't See That Coming...

2016 is well-documented in my journal. My little Nick was three, going on four, and no longer in speech therapy. He graduated before the New Year, and we were having plenty of little conversations. Life seemed normal, for the most part, despite his asthma that we were now getting under control. Here I sat, a stay-at-home mom keeping her kids preoccupied, with a husband who worked hard and was moving up in his company, getting yearly raises and incentives to give his little family every opportunity. We lived in an adorable house in the suburbs, with a huge fenced yard, the same one we bought from his parents when the economy crashed, with so much potential it almost hurt to think about. Even though we weren't really part of the community—because how can you be in a very LDS neighborhood in the center of Utah when you don't attend church?—Aryn had her friends, and Nick had an active momma who took him everywhere she went.

RAISED BY NARCOTICS—I Didn't See That Coming

While some things were getting better, I just felt tired—all the time. I had been to see my doctor to have several tests done the year previously to rule out why I was always tired, and for the first time he had me sit down and take a depression test. I passed, which is to say, I failed. I was depressed, and it was obvious. I had just been holding everything inside. My life was getting pieced back together, but I was in a constant state of depression, something for me that just felt normal. I didn't know anything else existed.

Let's go backwards a little, to August 2015. I started having severe headaches, only on the right side of my head, that were so painful and lasted for hours, but I—of course—refused to take anything for them. It felt like someone was jabbing a knife into my brain. It would leave me in tears, but after looking online at the different types of headaches people get, I didn't think it was typical of a migraine. I decided for myself that it was cluster headaches. My doctor told me it was migraines, but I didn't get sick having them, and I didn't feel the need to run away from light—if anything, sitting in the sun helped me feel better, as did having the light shine on my skin and breathing in the fresh air. A common method of treatment for cluster headaches is oxygen therapy. Not saying that stepping outside provided the amount of oxygen needed to qualify as oxygen therapy, but it definitely helped me feel better.

I thought I was dying. My doctor had me get two kinds of MRI scans to make sure it wasn't anything serious. I spent over $1,000 to come back with negative results. Spending that kind of money, you almost want to have something to show for it—but I had nothing, and I guess I was happy to not be dying.

With that on top of my depression—which I wasn't facing at that time—he prescribed me an antidepressant that doubled as a migraine reducer. He was convinced it was migraines. Okay, I didn't really care to keep spending money to figure it out. (BTW, I still get them.)

I took the medication for a few weeks. And I almost killed myself. I wanted it desperately. Something changed inside of me, and no matter how good my life was getting, and the work I was doing to keep it all together, I felt like I was back to square one. I just wanted to end it, and not even the thought of my little boy was going to persuade me otherwise.

I was scared.

I told Shawn. I had to. My life wasn't in my hands anymore.

Together, we threw away the medication, knowing it was the cause of my sudden suicidal thoughts.

I never told my doctor.

I stopped trusting him.

He didn't give me a reason to see a therapist, just handed me medication for migraines that would double as happy pills. I knew that I shouldn't have taken them. I don't take medication on principle. Medication killed my family. Narcotics killed my family and made my mother the crazy person she was. No way, keep that shit away from me.

But I wanted to feel better for my family, and as a result, they almost lost me. Again. I had to stop doing that.

RAISED BY NARCOTICS—I Didn't See That Coming

So, in 2016, I made the decision to use natural alternatives for everything from depression, to my headaches, to any disease I might run into as I turned thirty and kept getting older and older. I would not let age and illness ruin my chances at a long and healthy life with my family.

I signed up to become a certified health coach. That meant learning everything I could about nutrition and how it affected our health and well-being. How many things in my family's lives could have been different if they had just simply taken care of themselves? Eaten more fruits and vegetables, and been more active? I was angry at doctors for not prescribing a healthier diet and lifestyle, and now I would be the person in the world to help people overcome their illness through nutrition and activity. That desire expanded into ideas of being a yoga instructor or a physical therapist. I wanted to be able to truly help people like my family who were bogged down by the idea of their illness or disability. I wanted to help people overcome their battles with life through natural sources, not the self-medication that destroyed their family.

So, I focused on that, and gave it everything I had. I turned my own depression around, or so I thought, with the focus on my studies. And I kept pursuing a healthier alternative for myself through running and a whole foods diet.

Truthfully, I am still incredibly passionate about this. I believe that if we just focused on better nutrition, we would be healthier as a nation overall—but I learned the hard way that people don't want to be told how to eat or who to be or what to look like. We now live in a world where accepting your largeness as beautiful is the right thing to do, despite what health issues you will face as a result later in life. I'm all for accepting people of all shapes and sizes, but some sizes do come with consequences. No one wants to hear that, though. The only people who supported the idea of me being their health coach did so to support the dream I was building, not to turn their health around. I guess that's sweet.

That was my focus during 2016. That was going to be how I helped change the world. Little did I know I would sit down to have a conversation with a friend that would change all of it. Little did I know I would find myself sitting down at my computer, yet again, to find the words to share with the world about the experiences I've gone through, and what comes after.

What I didn't know during that time was one of my closest friends, Michelle, was going through something equally devastating in her own life. She and I are both very introverted, so we hardly see each other. When we do, our conversations are very profound—and long. I really enjoy this about her. Shawn and I had gone to their house for dinner one winter evening in December. After dinner she pulled me aside into her new office, which was something she had been hoping to create for herself for several years and had finally managed to do after their move into a bigger apartment. She admitted to me what was happening in her personal life, and that she had been seeing a therapist as a result. She told me that it was something she should have done before the problems started. I had already guessed at the problems before she sat down and admitted them to me. I've known her nearly as long as I've known Shawn, and in all those years, I knew she struggled with bouts of depression and would come and go from people's lives. This past summer she had vanished from social media and dropped everyone out of the blue, then came back a few months later with posts about "getting through the darkness." There were the vague, yet depressing, posts about her hardships in life.

While she and I sat chatting that evening, something happened to me that hadn't happened in a while. My legs seized up and started shaking. It was winter, but this wasn't happening because I was cold—I was having an anxiety attack. I told her as much. I knew the conversation was doing it to me, because I had known for years that I needed to see a therapist—or just get help of some sort. I needed to be able to talk about what was happening in my life to someone, and she sat and listened as I finally broke down the pieces of my life that had been killing me. I didn't go into depth—the way I might with a therapist, or the way she had with me just moments before—but she listened and encouraged me to find one. She helped me think outside of the box and use the resources I had to find one. And even if I did find one, she told me, it might take a while to find the *right* one.

I went home thinking hard about this. I thought I was doing the right things by taking care of myself and my nutrition. I was still running races and doing everything I could to focus on my health. Physically I was doing amazing, but what my conversation with her made me realize was that mentally I was not put together. By simply listening to her experiences in therapy, I nearly shook right out of my own body from the anxiety it was causing me to suppress every emotion I was having.

I knew, somewhere deep inside of my bones, that this focus I had placed on my physical wellbeing wasn't enough. It could alleviate some of the symptoms I faced as a person with depression, but I was also using it to run away from the emotional state I was in. This had been my first clue that I was dealing with something so fundamental to who I was that I didn't recognize it as something that could bubble up and tear me apart one day.

When I got home, I pulled up the website that was connected to our health insurance. Shawn had shown me how to look for doctors in our area that would be covered under our insurance. It was a very useful little tool. It gave a rundown of predicted pricing for various types of doctors, and I had used it a month earlier to find a new pediatrician for Nick and his asthma.

I looked for a woman, because men intimidated me, and I found one nearby. I found a few and I sent emails. I wasn't good with spoken words, so I hated calling. I was much better at writing it all out, so I did it once, and copy pasted it to see what kind of a response I was going to get.

Once I got a reply, I knew there was no turning back. I told Shawn what I was up to, and I looked deep inside of myself for courage.

Jenni V. was the first person to respond to me. She expressed her concern for me over my email and reassured me that she was experienced in specific areas such as trauma, depression, and anxiety. She said that she would like to sit down with me, and asked when it was most convenient for me. Once the conversation started, it was easy for me to feel like I was doing the right thing. She seemed friendly and easygoing, so we set up a time in the evenings once a week to see each other. Walking into my first appointment with her, I kept telling myself: *Breathe, this is going to be okay. You need this. This is the first step towards the rest of your life. Hopefully now you'll really be okay.* That chanting to myself didn't stop me from having anxiety from the moment I sat down until the moment I got home, but I was reassured by the presence of other people in the office with me. Was that what support looked like? Twiddling your thumbs while you wait for this person in your life to sort their shit out? I wondered to myself what they were going through and tried to just stare at my phone so as not to be totally obvious that I was curious about them, as I'm sure they were curious about me as well. I realized then and there that I would tell anyone my whole story if only they would ask me. I wanted to, I needed to . . . and now I had to pay someone to listen. That was going to have to be okay. I needed to be okay with that. As I sat there, I started making assumptions about the result of therapy. I would need to talk about everything, but I didn't know if I was ready to face the answers, one of which would be leaving Shawn and starting a new life on my own.

What was I really doing here? And was I ready to take the next big steps in my life to solve the problems I was having?

CHAPTER 31

What I Learned in Therapy

I have a tendency to symbolize everything in my life. I need to find a way to create meaning in everything I do, or it's simply not worth doing. The summer before I started therapy, I turned the big three zero. Thirty. For my thirtieth celebration, I wanted a great deal of things to celebrate. I wanted my friends and I go to Las Vegas together. One of them was only a week younger, and of course there was Mandy, whose birthday was a month before mine. It made sense to me to celebrate with the people I loved—or who I was trying to connect with, anyway. I mentioned it a few times, but everyone got busy doing other things. When I realized what was happening, I planned something else, something just for me. A half-marathon that would land about two weeks outside of my birthday. Something I could use to congratulate myself that I had made it this far in life, while also recognizing my physical strengths and everything I had worked for to be able to run distances like that. It was motivation to keep me running, something I could

RAISED BY NARCOTICS—What I Learned in Therapy

do for myself, and also something where I could force my family to come celebrate this milestone with me.

But that was just it. I was forcing them. Not long after I created the Facebook event inviting everyone to come high-five me at the finish line, I deleted the event and canceled on everyone, feeling sorry for myself that I had to throw my own birthday party and force people to stand around waiting for me when they probably didn't want to be there at all. It was a lot of overthinking, and a lot of anxiety. I wanted to be loved and cared for and supported, but I didn't want to have to force everyone in my life to be there for me. Why wasn't anyone planning this for me? Where were my best friends throwing me a dirty thirty birthday bash in Vegas? Where was my family creating a Facebook event in my honor to celebrate my big day with me?

Why was I doing this to myself?
Why did it all matter?
What was I proving?
Who cared?

I realized in that moment that I had absolutely nothing to prove to anyone. I had no parents to be proud of me or want me to feel special. I had become "Shawn's wife"—no one actually referred to me as myself. I was just an extension of the man I had married, maybe rightfully so. Was it really my own life I was living, anyway? I was supporting him in his dreams and making sure his life didn't fall apart by being the person who kept his children alive—the children who only ever had any resemblance to his side of the family, never my own. It was me who made sure the accounts were budgeted, and the bills were paid, and the dinners were being served. I kept his life together, but what about mine? I wasn't really any better than I had been two or three years earlier. I had just been hiding it from myself. What I didn't realize in that moment was how blind I still was to so much in my own life.

When the day came that I would finally sit down with Jenni—this person I had paid to be in my life, who I quickly realized was someone who seemed to click with me, who was patient and kind and guided me through the process, asking the right questions when they needed to be asked, and pausing me when she noticed that I was steering toward a problem I didn't recognize—so many things in my life started to fall into place.

The puzzle of who I was, and what my life had been all about, started piecing itself together. But I soon found an answer I never wanted.

The first thing she explained to me, in our very first session, was fight, flight, or freeze. We are all familiar with fight or flight, and my tendencies in life leaned heavily toward flight. I would fight when necessary, but I very much preferred to run away from my problems. I wanted escape so badly it hurt, in an almost physical way. I was always looking for a way out of where I was. What I hadn't known about was the "freeze."

Now typically this happens in response to a traumatic event—like rape, or a car accident, or something where you're about to experience severe injury. It's where you feel there is no hope of survival, and shut down physically,

RAISED BY NARCOTICS—What I Learned in Therapy

sometimes shutting out any memory of the event even happening. She related this to what I had been going through, specifically in what I considered my "shut down" years where I interacted with people only very minimally because nothing mattered beyond that. I had told her that I had these weird moments of forgetting everything that was happening around me, even while it was happening. This unfortunately still happens, and maybe other therapists could pick apart my brain even more and suggest other behavioral patterns for what I've been through. But as Jenni explained it, it kind of clicked. As people talked to me, I would shut out everything they said—go blank, so to speak—and have to either ask what they had just said, or just nod and walk away. The timeline of my life wasn't matching up, and still to this day, I swear I've added a blank year of complete nothing that doesn't even exist, but I'm nearly positive that I lived through it. I added a year somewhere between 2015 and 2016, making up a block of time that doesn't really exist anywhere. But it still stays dark inside of my head, as if a part of me is living there, but she's not really doing anything. I swear to God I must be crazy. I know it's not real, but it's real to me.

In essence, some part of me froze and stopped responding to reality, and I've lived in that, blocking out the day-to-day occurrences because I couldn't fight anymore. But neither could I flee, so I just stopped functioning, creating periods of darkness in my memory. That resonated within me.

What I had not realized, until years after Mom died, was that I lived through years of trauma and abuse, and most of my reactions to my current reality, no matter how great my new life was, was based on the fear that I would be abused again.

I am a whipped puppy, one who's been adopted into a new family but still clinging to old habits formed in an abusive situation. I have a dog like that now, and she hoards her food; she won't let my other dog eat it. She still shies away from my hand when I kneel down to pet her, sometimes running away from me several times, until she's brave enough to come back. She can see that I'm not abusing our other dog, and he's perfectly happy. My heart really goes out to her. I understand her. I wish I could tell her it was all okay.

What have you been through, my sweet little Lady?

These therapy sessions changed my life. It enabled me to look at how I responded to everything around me and start analyzing the "why" behind those reactions. She asked me questions like, "What would you tell them now? If they were putting you through that situation, and you had the frame of reference you do as an adult, what would you say to them? What would you do differently?"

Those questions fueled the fire to write this book. To really sit down and think about everything I had gone through, and how on earth I could ever help anyone else in a similar situation, because I know there are people who have experienced (or are experiencing) the same thing. *Lots* of people, and people in much worse situations.

RAISED BY NARCOTICS—What I Learned in Therapy

My story is not meant to be a sob story, or "that poor girl and all she went through." I hope that by sharing my story, even if you don't really care about me, you will care about the person you know who is living through the same hell.

Read my words, hear my words, and know that you know someone in this exact situation. Don't feel bad for me—help them.

I have one more thing to say about therapy. When you start therapy, you often wonder to yourself: "When will I know that I'm done being in therapy? How long is this going to last?"

For some, maybe most, you just stop having things to talk about. I don't know, actually. I kind of assumed that would be how it works.

I know for myself that I could potentially be in therapy for years, but I had a moment with this therapist—not because of her, but because of a realization she helped me have—that changed the way I viewed everything I experienced in my life, and not for the better. But it was the one thing that made me stop looking for answers, because where can you really go from there? Everything I felt had been wrong. Had I put myself through hell all these years for nothing?

CHAPTER 32

Drug Addict

Human memory is incredibly fallible, and it's this moment that makes this story hard to write, because it throws into question everything I thought I knew about how I grew up. While reading this story, you've likely already made the connections that it took me years to put together. Before therapy, I assumed a lot of things about my own mother, things that I might have a different perspective on than, say Cody. But we agree on some of those perspectives, like the chance that she, too, was bipolar or potentially schizophrenic like her sister Teresa—especially given hallucinations seeing and hearing dead people communicating with her, and her constant mood swings that included hiding from people when she was upset, literally locking the door and refusing to interact with anyone.

Michelle—the same person who watched Aryn the night that my mother passed, the one who encouraged me into therapy and helped me realize the traumatic life I've

RAISED BY NARCOTICS—Drug Addict

led—said to me once, over a casual conversation at a local coffee shop, "You can't write your story until you've finished living it." A profound statement that I sat with for a long time. Was I finished living my story, enough to put it into words on paper, like I had continuously tried and failed to do? No, I mean, I'm far from dead yet. I'm only thirty-two right now, so assuming I don't die young in a tragic accident or health problem, I have quite a few years left to live. Good ones, too, I hope. So, when did I realize that my story was ready to be written?

The day I realized that my mother was a drug addict.

The realization happened slowly, in a therapy session that was nearing the end of its hour. My therapist had worked with people on the streets of Salt Lake City and had easily pieced together the very thing I had lived my life in denial over. I had finally gotten to the part of my story where Mom had been in a shelter, and I hadn't known what to do. We had been given the runaround at her doctor's office and very likely Mom had thrown out the papers that I had tried so hard to get for her—the papers to get her the help she needed. Mom had gone missing and had weird stories of strange men when she returned. Old friends coming out of the woodwork to break into our old home on Nebo Drive to steal Mom's prescription meds. The fact that Mom never tried very hard to be a real member of society, and was always asking for cash, and sometimes refusing the help I could offer instead. Her mood swings from incredible anger to incredible calm. Her "remission"—as she described it—from the illness that was slowly killing her, robbing her of her ability to remember what day it was, or where she was.

My therapist let me come to my own conclusions, and when it hit me, it hit hard—and I had the worst panic attack I had ever experienced in my entire life, right there in front of her, as she tried to ground me and help me out of it. Her other patients were waiting and probably listening to my hysterics just outside the door to her office.

Mom had been a drug addict

Not just a prescription drug addict, although that's likely where it started, and what she lived for. No, there was a lot of evidence that pointed directly to heroin, including the scars all over Mom's arms and face, the one's she attributed to lupus. The skeletal figure I remember seeing in the final months, when Steve was magically appearing in her life. I saw through the perfect illusion she was creating for me the entire time.

Every single memory I had of her since I was about thirteen, maybe even before, exploded in my face. Shards of lies spreading across my vision, and I couldn't handle it anymore. Had Mom even had lupus? Or was that a lie to cover up the fact that she had gotten addicted to Teresa's pain killers? Was lupus how she was able to doctor-shop and hitch her own ride through the dark land of drug addiction? Had her doctor known, and was that why he had been silent with me all those years before?

I can't possibly believe that Mom's lupus was a lie, but I tell you this now to showcase the very real issue I came up

RAISED BY NARCOTICS—Drug Addict

against in realizing that Mom was so much more than just a woman succumbing to her disease.

At every memory, I burst into tears anew, not being able to handle the sudden light at the end of a very dark tunnel I had been walking through. Answers started to fall through a door that I had kept locked for so many years of my life, unwilling to even acknowledge existed—yet, now that I knew, it seemed painfully obvious. Take, for instance, when I took her to see Dr. Bennet, and he pretty much brushed me off. Now I wondered why? Why didn't he seem more concerned? Did he know and think I was an idiot for trying to cover it up for her, when in reality I was completely clueless? Is that why she didn't know what day it was?

Everyone knew that Teresa had been addicted to her painkillers. There was no secret there, and it was devastating when she passed away because no one had even tried to help her have any real or meaningful long-term solutions for her life. Teresa was mentally ill, and when she had sleepovers with her girlfriends, we all knew that she was abusing alcohol (and potentially more). But had she been the one to open those doors for Mom, or had Mom used her to gain access to her lifestyle? Did every adult in my life try to shelter me from the truth they thought they would take to their graves?

The information was too much for me to handle. She had been a mother, my mother, and mothers don't do heroin! And yet Jenni V. was confirming every fear I was having by explaining to me that she had witnessed this same struggle in so many others, and there was good reason to believe that when Mom had gone missing, she was searching for drugs.

What about that night when she became homeless because of whatever Steve had done to her? Or with her? What had she put herself through? She loved her homeless family and didn't ask to come back. She asked for money, and although I sent care packages, she was always disappointed when I didn't just send money instead. Had she been on those kinds of drugs when she was caring for my daughter while I was finishing school? Were those the moments that she tried to become clean, and went into "remission" because she was trying to be a good Nana?

Goddamn it, Mom!

Those outbursts at Christmas, was that because she just needed to get away to her stash, and get another hit?

Too much.

I couldn't bear it.

I tried my best to calm myself. I had to go pick up Nick from his preschool class now that my appointments were during his class time. I was a complete mess. I used my sunglasses to shade my eyes so the other moms there wouldn't know what I had just gone through or ask questions.

"Are you okay?" They never asked this—this was just a scenario in my head that I desperately wanted to avoid.

No.

No, I'm not fucking okay.

RAISED BY NARCOTICS—Drug Addict

I just realized my mother was a goddamn drug addict, probably using heroin to self-medicate, and that's why she couldn't pay her rent on her apartment even though she should have had enough money to do so, and kept running away to get more, but she's been dead for nearly five years and oh my god, that's how she died, a drug overdose, just like Teresa.

Just a minute, just one goddamn minute . . .

I fought myself and the internal dialogue running through my head.

Teresa had died of a drug overdose, a stroke that killed her in her sleep when she had over medicated. I had wondered how Mom was keeping her lupus at bay when she had been homeless and living in that shelter, and now it was clear to me exactly how she died . . .

Except . . .

I would truly never know the truth about anything she went through.

I would never know the woman who brought me into the world.

Everything I thought I knew—a complete lie.

And then it got worse.

Jo called me shortly after I got home with Nick and Aryn. I had been pacing my kitchen, calling Cody, telling him what had happened, listening to him deny the truth behind what I saw.

"No, she wasn't a drug addict, Alyse, she had lupus," he stated.

I understood why he couldn't see it—I didn't want to see it, even now—but it was there, and every memory was shifting in my head, turning into lies I didn't want to live with. Then Jo called, wanting to come over and drop a few things off before their next big vacation somewhere. It wasn't a good time, but when else would they have the chance?

"Sure, you can come over," I told her.

I hoped it was quick. I wanted to crumble. I'm sure my face was red, and my eyes were bloodshot from crying like a lunatic, but I still hoped they would just let me say I was okay when they asked, "How are you doing?"

But I saw it in her eyes—she knew I wasn't okay the minute she opened the door.

"I can stay for a few minutes and you can talk to me?" she said in a question, leaving it up to me. She grabbed my hand and led me to my safe place.

She ended up staying for two hours, while we talked in the sunshine on the front porch of my home, Grandpa Ray happily entertaining his two grandkids, never asking what was going on, or coming out to rush us to end our conversation. In that conversation, Jo opened up to me about something.

"I went to see your Mom," she said, "after you two had trouble finding her help. I sat with her, and I offered her a place to stay in the assisted living center that we owned. I told her I would help her get the best medical care, and take her to see my doctors, but Alyse, honey, she said no. She flat

RAISED BY NARCOTICS—Drug Addict

out refused me, and told me that she just wanted the money, and then asked me to leave."

That confirmed it for me. That was it. Mom had the chance to start over, get the medical care she couldn't afford with the help of my rich family—the very same family that she resented me for being a part of because I wouldn't give her their money. That was enough to make me believe that what I thought I knew now was absolutely the truth.

When someone has lupus, they typically form a rash. It's called a butterfly rash and it spreads across their nose and cheeks. They also have a very strong sensitivity to sunlight, having to cover up their skin and not stay outdoors for very long before their skin blisters.

Heroin addicts have obvious scars from where they inject the drugs into their system—from there, they become skeletal. Their eyes become hollow, their cheekbones protrude, and they develop scabs on their face and the rest of their body—as if they had scraped themselves up, and it just started to heal over.

Mom's scars resembled that of a heroin addict.

It doesn't help now that about a month ago I did a Google search online for "heroine face scars" to see if they resembled what Mom looked like at her worst. I have photos, damn it, I have evidence of this. They do resemble what she looked like.

But again, I will just never know the truth. I never can. She's gone and gone is anyone else who could confirm or deny what she went through. When she died, no doctor told me whether they had done drug testing. Why would they?

Would they have thought to? I don't know. I can't know. There are too many variables here for me to know what the truth is.

Some days I live in denial. Some days I tell myself that she just had a shitty life with shitty circumstances and she used what the doctors gave her to escape from it all. Some days I live with what I feel is the truth: after all the death in our family, she went looking for more to numb the additional pain in her heart, and escape from the reality she didn't want to live in.

I want to ask you a question now: does it really matter which one I believe? Either way, Mom was a drug addict. Whether it was to prescription drugs given to her by a doctor, or heroin she found on the street, or both.

What happened to me since discovering all of this through therapy? Well, first, I stopped going. I went a few more times afterward, but as I wrote in my journal, I found that I just didn't have it in me to keep going. Maybe I wanted to be in denial about what she had been through, and I opened a door to something I hadn't been ready to face, and I didn't want to risk doing that to myself again. What else don't I know? I don't really want to uncover it.

Second, it changed how I viewed my health, and the extreme efforts I had made in taking control of anything that could potentially go wrong within my body. I tried as hard as I could to not be anything like my mother—and I had assumed everything she had gone through was due to her poor health and the prescription drugs she had taken to alleviate her symptoms. Now, I still believe that I should do

RAISED BY NARCOTICS —Drug Addict

everything I can to avoid the world of prescription drugs, but I'm also a woman who believes in the benefits of science and the fact that what we have created can benefit us depending on the circumstances. All things in moderation. If you can avoid it, work to avoid it; if you can't, then work to minimize it. Why?

Because I do want to live.

I do not want to die, and I do not want to be bedridden—it has become my greatest fear.

For a long while, I stopped running. I stopped caring about what I ate, because it suddenly didn't matter. To avoid being like Mom, all I had to do was not do drugs, 'mkay. No longer did I need to fear any ailment I would come up against. I could and would be better about controlling any substance that came into my home, simply because of how I grew up.

I had lived in fear of so many things, but with this realization of Mom's choices, I was finally free of the guilt and the regret that I could have, or should have, done more.

My story is over. I am a free woman. No longer do I wish to harm myself because of the mistakes I've made in the past, the people that I've hurt, the abuse that I survived, and the person I'm afraid to become. This is the freest I have ever felt in my life. Finally, I can write my story.

But my story is far from over.

CHAPTER 33

I Wish

I can't help but wonder: what would Mom think about all of this? Would she be proud? Would she be embarrassed? Would she finally feel that her existence on this planet meant something?

All three of the women who raised me are now dead. Each one leaving a profound hole inside of my heart—and each of those holes, over the years, have filled with fragments of pain, love, regret, acceptance, loneliness, and a deep yearning for change.

When Teresa died, I dreamed about her often. In those dreams she was always sitting downstairs, and just about to tell me something amazing or life-altering, and I would try to walk to her, to hug her, but either the dream would fade, or I would wake up.

When Grandma Jane passed away—really the only normal death of the three women—everything outdoors reminded me of her. The flowers, the mountains, the wonderful wildlife. She seemed to exist in nature, and still

RAISED BY NARCOTICS — I Wish

does. That's where I meet her when I need her strength. It has become one of the most important things in my life, the ability to go outside, anywhere, and enjoy the beauty of nature the way she would have appreciated it.

When Mom died, two things happened: for the first year or more when I dreamed of her, she was always yelling at me or trying to kill me. What's funny about these dreams is that she herself had a dream interpretation book, and sometimes we would sit for hours picking apart what they meant. She did this for everyone who was willing to sit with her. What did you mean, Mom, when you were trying to kill me in my dreams?

The second thing that started happening were the long phone conversations in my dreams. Over the years they became in person, like I was getting to know my mom on a new level, in a new way, the new her. Occasionally, and this still occurs, I see people who look like her and I think for a minute that it is her. I let myself live in that moment and pretend she's still here, and that if she saw me she would be happy, and we would start up a fun conversation or laugh over something.

What I know is how badly I miss them all. Sure, we had it rough, but it wasn't always like that—we had our great times together too, where we all laughed so hard we cried. I miss those moments the most, and I miss what we were never able to have: a future together.

* * *

Drugs—prescription and otherwise—took from my family the chance we all had at a normal life. A life of hopes and dreams, and really just time together enjoying each other.

Time is the one thing I value most in this life, and the one thing that drugs took from my family.

By the time I was twenty-five, my family was dead. One day, I had the realization that I would spend the rest of my life never being able to see them or talk to them ever again. It's not necessarily something you actively think about, or even know, but when it finally hits you, it's devastating.

Once Mom died, and a few years later when I realized I would never be able to go home again, never see their faces . . . the grief started anew, like it had all just happened again.

I miss my Mom.

I miss my Aunt Teresa.

I miss my Grandma Jane.

I miss the crazy life we had together.

I am an abused puppy who wishes she could go back to her former situation, and just see if this time it could be different, if this time they'll reach down and pet me.

I wish for a time when the accident never happened, and drugs never came into our home the way they did.

I wish, I wish, I wish . . .

All I have left is a story full of people who loved me and made mistakes. People who didn't know where to turn for answers to solve the problems in their lives, but I can't say

RAISED BY NARCOTICS—I Wish

they didn't try. Each one of them tried, even Teresa. They didn't want to be who they were becoming, and they certainly didn't want to lose their lives and never have a chance to try again.

I'm so angry for each one of them.

I'm angry for myself.

Even if all our circumstances had been exactly the same, the outcome did not need to be their deaths.

CHAPTER 34

That's It

Drugs and medicines have been around for all of human history. They're just plants, really. That we use or even abuse drugs is not new to our humanity, or any culture therein. Shawn was the one to bring this bit of information to my ears recently, and I feel it's incredibly important to share, especially here at the end of this book. Even though we have used drugs for so long, we are the first generation in recorded human history to kill ourselves off in such an epidemic of drug overdoses. More and more grandparents across our country are having to step up and become legal guardians of their grandchildren because an entire generation is dying. Why?

Look at how I grew up—this could be any one of us. Remove my name from this book and you could very easily replace it with any number of people struggling with very similar stories. I've said it before and I'll say it again: this isn't news to any of us. We know what's happening, but we don't know how to fight it. It doesn't even matter what your

RAISED BY NARCOTICS—That's It

background is, how poor or rich you might be. This is literally affecting every walk of life.

It's here that I think about the tobacco industry. People within the walls of Big Tobacco have been known to say that it's all part of "natural selection." We knew, have known, how terrible cigarettes are for us, and yet there are so many of us who refuse to quit. Now, we have a similar and maybe even more deadly issue with Big Pharma and the myriad of pills we use to suppress every single hardship in our lives. We have come to rely on our drugs/medicines, both over-the-counter and prescription, to essentially solve our problems, big and small. Everything from insomnia and sadness to major debilitating illness or injury.

We are a generation of people who do not know the first thing about facing our difficulties in life and overcoming them. This is not to belittle our generation—this is to aid future generations and get ours to stop dying. Guys, we're dying. We're losing. I couldn't tell you who's winning, but we are definitely losing.

Throughout my life, I've felt victimized and resentful towards the people in my life and the circumstances in which I've lived. How much was in my control? Not much, realistically—almost nothing. What could I have really done differently to try to save my family, short of finding a mad scientist to create a time machine to go back and warn them? If only. Everything my family did was in an effort to heal. To put back together the very literal, broken pieces of ourselves. We were taught that what we were doing was the right choice. We were given what we knew to be solutions to help us live fuller, longer lives, but ultimately it cost us our lives. Now we are finally learning the true effects of these drugs that were meant to be an answer to our problems. Now, they *are* our problems.

We use our pain to create change, and in writing this book, I believe you can now see that I'm in great pain. My pain has not gone away. I don't want my pain to go away. I don't want to hide from my pain anymore. I don't want anyone else to hide from their pain, either. Life is painful, in so many ways, but it is with that pain that great change can be accomplished. If we never felt pain, we would never have come as far as we have as a species, culture, nation . . . whatever you want to call us, this large entity of people. This right here is why I'm optimistic about our futures, because we are in pain.

Politically, there are insurmountable problems we must overcome. I'm not here to be political, because I don't feel that it's necessary, however much I would love to see some serious reform within the medical and pharmaceutical industries. I would love to see the cost of healthcare drop dramatically. I would love to see up-front pricing options across the board, standardized payments no matter who you are, where you live, or what your ailment. My son's medication for his asthma ranges anywhere from $150-$400 per month depending on what insurance you do or do not have, who your doctor is, where you live in this country, etc. So many factors playing the part in what is a very bogus number almost literally pulled out of someone's ass.

RAISED BY NARCOTICS—That's It

But I want to hand these problems over to people who are more politically inclined. People who feel passionate about law and reform. What I'm passionate about is and always will be humanity. I truly believe that despite whatever government you live under, you have more freedoms than you will ever realize, especially in our great nation of America. We have the freedom to create our own change, whether whatever current president says we can or cannot. I didn't need a law to be passed for me to write and release this book. Yes, I know, not all countries are as free as ours, but there are people in those countries who are facing their own pains and creating the change they need. Just as we will here.

This is a spider web. One person's decision has far reaching effects that ripple off in millions of directions. Just like Teresa's accident, which caused my family to spiral into what it became—that all started with one person completely disconnected from my family making a choice that caused them to fall asleep behind the wheel and run into the side of Grandma Jane's car. Just as that one person created turmoil within my family, so too can I cause disruption with this book. This book is a result of that long-ago decision, and we can't say just how far reaching these actions and words will be from this point forward.

There are so many pieces of this book that I feel I need to tie into this last chapter. I have felt incredibly out of control in my life, even now. I can't change any of the decisions that my family made, beginning with my mother and a father who chose to abandon me. Maybe I really am a product of Mom's decision to trap Ben into staying with an unplanned pregnancy. No matter how I came into the world, I can't change that. She, at least, stayed. She raised me, and for a long time—ten years, which on the cosmic scale is almost nothing—she was a great role model for me and what it meant to have strength and overcome your obstacles. She told me once that she should have given me up for adoption, something that I was very angry about when she said it, but now as I look at it, she only wanted me to have the life she knew she could never give me, because what she could give me was pain. But without that pain, where's the change? I don't regret my life. I don't regret having gone through any of what I saw or what I experienced. I don't regret my pain.

Inherently we see pain as a negative, not a positive. Could we ever change that? I hope to. The pains we feel in life—stress, anxiety, depression, illness and injury—we hide from. We want them gone. They are incredibly uncomfortable, and I don't know about you, but for me it's also been a little bit embarrassing. It's that shame we feel that pushes us into things like suicide or self-injury or self-medication. But could we work around it? Could we be a little more forgiving of the people around us and their pains in life? Could we even try to understand it? Maybe not, but we can understand the fact that they are suffering, and that in our suffering what we need most are other people to listen and support us. We could erase the stigma and be more forthcoming with our pain so that those around us can support us. Support. A network of people. Community. Family.

RAISED BY NARCOTICS—That's It

We've created a structure for our society, and unless you fit within the walls of that structure, you are, by default, failing. You are a failure. Here, have a drug to overcome it, it's the only way.

Bullshit.

So, what now?

Well, honestly, since no one else seems to want to do it, I create the change I wish to see in the world. I create the family that I never had. You and me, we're family now, and you're going to be here for me, and I'm going to be here for you. We are going to fucking support each other.

Can it be that simple? Why the hell not?

Let's find out.

Support is it. That's what this was all about. This is the thing we all need, and again, I say for the hundredth time, this is not news to anyone. Pay it forward, as it were. We are good people, you are a good person. Maybe you're angry, maybe you're hurt, maybe you need support so you can support the people in your life. Reach out to one person. Reach out both for help and to be the support someone else needs.

This isn't the end of my story, but it is time to put the book down and do something about the story that has become all too common in all our lives.

ACKNOWLEDGMENTS

It takes a village to write a book. Although I may have written the memories down on my own, I had many people who loved me, supported me, held my hand during dark times, accepted my absence when I felt lost and shared their own memories, sorrow, and joy with me on this long journey.

Thank you to my family Shawn, Aryn, Nicolas, Amanda, and Cody for being everything I never knew I needed in life. You are all my heroes, and I am inspired daily by your combined courage, strength, humor, creativity and kindness.

Thank you to my editors Julie, Keith, and Michelle for helping me to shape this book into something the world will want to hold in their hands. It's a huge accomplishment in my eyes to not only write a book, but pick it apart, take a step back, see the bigger picture and put it all back together again.

Thank you to my family and friends who have patiently waited and supported this crazy idea of mine to write this book. You guys believed in me when it really mattered, and I am eternally grateful.

Many many more thanks to every single person who has ever touched my life. You may never know your true worth, but I can tell you that it is profound.

YOU ARE NOT ALONE

Visit the Bottled Up Foundation at:
bottledupfoundation.org

and on Facebook at:
facebook.com/groups/bottledup

www.ingramcontent.com/pod-product-compliance
Lightning Source LLC
Chambersburg PA
CBHW021356290426
44108CB00010B/267